All proceeds from the sale of
this book will be used to fund
continued improvements at
Still Waters Retreat Center.

"Rarely does an author have the courage to tell her personal story just as it is. Too often there is a hidden agenda but Amy tells a different story. She shares what has actually happened in the living present of a woman, partner, artist and spiritual soul who takes up life's most difficult and important questions and grinds them out through the thick and thin unfolding of a life. There are no easy pieces in this account of a woman, brave enough to be herself, time after time as she witnesses her own imperfections. In this era of entitlement and celebrity, it is often too easy to imagine human life as a progression from good hard work to the rewards we have been promised. In our hearts, we know, at least for ourselves, life isn't like that. We stretch, we reach and we dig deeper inside ourselves when outside everything is falling apart. That's how we are. Imperfect even at the core. People don't want to admit this. Much less people on a self-improvement spiritual path. But it's true. We need to settle ourselves with this. When we come home to the simple naked truth of our existence, we reflect in the way Amy has reflected here. Transparent truth heals both the speaker and the listener.

Some might think this is a story about alcohol addiction. It is not. Some might think this is a story about an artist coming to terms with her gifts. It is not. Some might think it is a rather parochial biopic about life in a small city in central CT or the struggles of two people falling in love with each other, stitching together a dream called Still Waters. It is not.

It is a story of being human, just as we know we are, and just as we fear we are. Nothing more, nothing less. Reading this book demands something of our attention. It tells us that most of the time, we are unable to speak of the real life of being who we are. Simply that. It is our naked truth that is hardest to speak. It takes an extraordinary voice to speak that truth. In this book, Amy speaks with this voice."

~ *Bonnitta Roy, Alderlore Insight Center*

Finding Still Waters

the art of
conscious
recovery

•

amy
labossiere

*Ian —
creativity heals
♡ Amy Lab.*

Still Waters Pond
Voluntown, CT

Image List:
All works by Amy LaBossiere unless noted otherwise.
To see full-color versions, visit amylabossiere.com

Crude Reality. 2004. Voluntown, CT.

Crude Reality II. 2016. Hartford, CT.

Legs. 2007. In Private Collection, West Hartford, CT.

Joey with Kidney Stones Healed. 2008. Hartford, CT.

Getting the Love You Want. 2008. Hartford, CT.

Self-Portrait, I Can Stop Anytime I Want. 2008.
In Private Collection, West Hartford, CT.

Death of Socrates. 1787. By Jacques-Louis David. Metropolitan Museum of Art. Catharine Lorillard Wolfe Collection, Wolfe Fund, 1931.
www.metmuseum.org/collection/the-collection-online/search/436105

Square One. 2009. In Private Collection.

Fibonacci Chakra Curve. 2009. In Private Collection.

River of Consciousness. 2009. In Private Collection.

In Keeping. 2009. In Private Collection of Tao LaBossiere.

Blank Slate. 2009. In Private Collection.

Process and View. 2009. In Private Collection.

Morphic Resonance. 2009. Hartford ArtSpace, Hartford, CT.

The Akashic Field. 2009. In Private Collection of Carol King.

Cubist Death of Socrates. 2009. In Private Collection.

A Sense of Being Stared At. 2010. In Private Collection, Hartford, CT.

I Know What You're Thinking. 2010. In Private Collection.

These Truths Are Self-Evident. 2010. In Private Collection.

Gemini Moon. 2010. Hartford ArtSpace, Hartford, CT.

Spiral Dynamics with Shadow Self. 2010. Hartford ArtSpace, Hartford, CT.

Summoning My Better Angels. 2010. In Private Collection.

Here, There Be Dragons. 2010. In Private Collection.

Transformation in Progress. 2010. In Private Collection.

My Oppression Ain't Pretty. 2010. In Private Collection.

Hooping the Spiralectic. 2010. Hartford ArtSpace, Hartford, CT.

Dedication

For my husband Tao
and Still Waters, the sacred land
for which we are shepherds

Foreword by Chris Grosso

There may be no greater understatement than that of "life is hard," and yet, it might be the one undeniable universal truth that we all share. Life is hard; it's so goddamn hard. It demands everything of us, but what happens when we're not ready, or able, to show up and offer life our entire everything? Speaking from my own experience, it breaks the heart. For some, this break may be a little, while for others, it may be a lot. For most of us, we're not even aware the break is happening. And this is very understandable as we're caught up in the business that is life, which makes perfect sense because it's what we've known our entire lives. That is until it doesn't make sense anymore.

I believe there are times in every single one of our lives where we have "moments of clarity." For some, it may be while staring down the barrel of a gun, while for others it might be while listening to a particular song, or teaching, creating art, hiking in nature, making love, skateboarding, or any of the other myriad ways in which life can surprise us. Whatever the cause, life is full of moments of clarity, or "awakening." And that's what Amy LaBossiere's Finding Still Waters is all about: cultivating those brief moments of awakening and clarity in a way that brings us to a place of greater compassion, loving-kindness, and connection with ourselves, with others, and with life as a whole.

There's a place within each of us, a place that for many seems hidden and mysterious, but it's there. This is the place where, when we experience those brief moments of clarity and awakening, life, in its most abstract and curious ways, makes perfect sense. It's as if in those fleeting moments we are able to see... no, feel... no, be... yes, be one with the Ultimate greatness that we call life. And when I say great, I mean great. It's HUGE — so huge in fact, that it contains the entire essence of you, and me, and quite literally, everything under, above and around the sun. That's right: Every. Single. Thing. It's so grand that it's incomprehensible by the rational mind. It completely defies it. Even as I sit here writing these words, it's still inconceivable to me as well. Yet, it's something that I, Amy, and many others have experienced time and again, in various ways, which has allowed us to know this complete and utter perfection of truth. But even that isn't a fair description as "various" is a word implying multiplicity, whereas this experience is singular. It's a singular that again, includes the sum total of all things, both seen and unseen.

There is a longing within every one of us. It plays out in different ways for individuals, but it's there. For many of us, it may result in turning to drugs, alcohol, sex, shopping, gambling or any of the other myriad ways human beings can distract themselves. And we turn to these things in a futile attempt to avoid our feelings of longing and the emptiness inside. (Amy, as did I, struggled with many of the aforementioned aversions.)

For others, they may turn to violence, gang affiliation, or again, any of the myriad ways that can make an individual feel as if they're in control of something. And it makes sense, doesn't it? Because we fear not being in control, and we fear being alone, and possibly worst of all, we fear feeling vulnerable, and these are awful fears. Who wants to feel beaten down or broken by life (regardless of the cause) in such a way that leaves us feeling vulnerable and exposed? Yet it's in these places of vulnerability that lays the most significant opportunity for personal growth. The reason is that it's in this place where we have little to no fight left, which makes it that much easier for us to begin laying aside our hearts armor. Once we're able to do that, our raw and vulnerable hearts are now exposed in a way that real growth and healing can begin. And from this place of internal growth and healing, we can then start to offer our best selves to the world, a self that can also be of tremendous service to others, rather than only looking out for our own best interest.

I spent many, many years only looking out for "mine." Turning to drugs and alcohol to find some relief from the overwhelming stress of day-to-day life. And let me say very clearly that I get it. I totally understand the relief drugs and alcohol (or any of the means mentioned above of aversion) can bring. When we're in that place of virtually unbearable pain, I completely understand how that temporary relief means more than the bigger picture; the larger scheme of life that lies ahead.

While recently speaking with Grammy Nominated Kirtan Musician Krishna Das, I asked him about this, explicitly addressing why, in his opinion, people turn to drugs? Why are we willing to compromise our best selves for a few moments, or hours, of relief when we know the potential consequences? His response was:

"Well, on one hand, who the fuck are we? Where the fuck are we? What the fuck are we doing? How did we get here? We've been shot out of a cannon, and we're hurtling through space, and we're trying to get comfortable. It's almost impossible. We're trying to find a place to land. I think people are just so lost, and so clueless, and so hurt that they need to numb themselves. They need to anesthetize themselves and self-medicate because how do you fucking deal with this? What is this? Even people who don't consciously ask that question are constantly running around trying to get money, trying to get jobs, trying to get pussy, trying to get cars, trying to get all kinds of stuff. They're compulsively doing all of this shit, completely not present, and there's a part of you that just has to stop. But they have no tools for that. Their parents didn't know about that. The people they grew up with didn't know about that. Nobody in their life knows about that, so the only thing they know is chemicals. Sleeping pills, alcohol, drugs, dangerous sports; anything that pulls us out of our mind and out of our suffering, no matter how temporarily, is what we're going to go for. And the problem, of course, is that none of that stuff really works, except temporarily. Maharajji said, "Go ahead into a room and smoke hash; the only problem is, it doesn't work. If it worked, I'd get a whole bunch of hash, we'd all go into a room, and we'd smoke together. But it doesn't work." So the problem is that people don't see it doesn't work because they don't understand that something else might be possible. That's the real killer — that most people will never have that conscious glimmer of real hope, or a real understanding that there's another way to be in the world. They won't even get a chance to ask the question. They will just tumble and roll until they hit the wall and die. When you really see this, this is how you develop compassion, because you see the state of things. You see how lucky you are that you know something even exists, to the tiny little infinitesimal percentage that you're able to know something. Still, it's enough to change the way we live and go through the day."

Krishna Das's questions, "Who the fuck are we? Where the fuck are we? What the fuck are we doing? How did we get here?" were among several I, and Amy, found ourselves desperately trying to answer throughout our healing journeys. For me, this ultimately led me back to a place of deep despair, depression, and isolation that resulted in yet another relapse to drugs and alcohol that very literally almost took my life. I found myself waking up in a jail cell in Hartford, CT after a blackout drunk experience only to be released the following morning on a P.T.A. (Promise To Appear). And right on schedule, as I walked out of the precinct into the hot and humid July summer morning in New England, the withdrawals began to set in, something that Amy, unfortunately, knows all too well about. But as she shares in Finding Still Waters, it doesn't have to be that way. Amen.

May this book serve to inspire those who read it towards greater love, compassion, kindness, acceptance, and peace. May we all come to know happiness and freedom from suffering. And may we all learn to love ourselves, and one another, without holding back.

- Chris Grosso, author of *Indie Spiritualist,*
  Everything Mind, and Dead Set On Living

Introduction

I wonder if someone becomes an alcoholic or is simply born that way. I've had my share of life events that I spent a lot of time avoiding and stuffing with alcohol and drugs. I had to find a new way to live or I was going to die.

This memoir shares my experience of growing up with love, trauma and uncertainty. I cannot possibly write all the stories I have within me. They are always piling up on themselves as I experience life, moment to moment. It is my hope that I have distilled this first batch well enough to make my stories enjoyable. Perhaps you will identify with some of the experiences or feelings. If you have ignored some deep creative calling, you might be ready to change that. Maybe it will inspire you to heal some pain or do something exciting in your life. It is my hope that the insights weaved through these chapters will entice you. Perhaps you will consider a path of emotional excavation and art making.

If you are in need of healing, you might find that too. Perhaps you are willing to take the hard journey of the spiritual path. For some of us, the choice is either the spiritual road or blotting our lives out in oblivion. I did the latter, somewhat unconsciously, for most of my adult life, until all the wine was too much and I was going to make myself very sick if I continued on that path.

Several years ago, I started to manage my elderly father-in-law Paul's care. I could not have expected that when the help he needed intensified, my writing voice would emerge again. "Hey, write this down. Hey, write about your experience. Hey, why don't you write and help some people with your words," my inner voice whispered.

At first, I thought this book was going to be about the care of Paul and all the miracles that I experienced. But then I thought deeply, why did this voice emerge? What is the message that wants to be shared? I realized that it was my sober, creative voice. My voice in recovery wants to be expressed — along with all the spiritual and soulful gifts delivered to me over the past years. I had to write it because maybe someone could benefit from this experience and might not have to endure the same pain or at least learn that there are tools to handle anything that life sends our way. It won't always make it better, but it might help us through.

No matter where this book brings you, I hope you find healing. I hope you find self-love and acceptance. I hope you find some ease and comfort without an excessive use of alcohol or drugs. I hope you see the beautiful aspects of life as they present themselves, in all their imperfect perfectness.

Part One: A Beginning

Chapter One:
Childhood + Other Devastations

♥

"I was learning that if I lived slightly
in the future — what will happen next —
I didn't have to feel so much about
what was going on in the present."

- Augusten Burroughs, *Running with Scissors*

Childhood + Other Devastations

My childhood memories are faint, sporadic glimmers in a fog of moments that might have happened. I don't know which are true or false. Some of my memories are from pictures. I see the picture in my mind's eye and hear the stories family members shared.

I grew up in New York on Long Island, the second daughter in a middle-class family. In my early childhood, my father was a high-powered, well-known corporate executive and my mother quit her job to be a stay-at-home mom.

We had a large yellow ranch home in Huntington, NY. Dad made sure we had a picture perfect front lawn. Every spring, the daffodils and forsythia would come up. It was pretty and well manicured. Our expansive backyard abutted a private Catholic High School. Near the border of the school, way in the back, we had a large sandbox and swing set. I would play out there and it seemed like the house was a mile away. Next to our house was a built-in swimming pool. One day, I stepped on a wasp and screamed my head off. To this day, I am deathly afraid of those creepy buggers.

We lived down the street from a famous football player, and Mom would have afternoon coffee with his wife and other neighbors. I called one of the neighbors Auntie, as she and Mom were best friends. Auntie was Jewish and an excellent cook. We'd go to her house for dinner of potato latkes, matzo and crispy, cold fried fish. My sister and I had grape juice while the adults drank Manichewitz wine or coffee.

When I was seven years old, my mother and father's relationship broke apart and they divorced. My father worked long hours in the corporate world. Mom said he didn't really want much to do with us kids when he got home. He wanted to have dinner, watch some TV and work on the yard. Mom said that didn't work for her. I think she was lonely and bored. I don't have the facts of what destroyed their marriage. Who knows what really happens in a relationship. Things are always pretty complex and there are two sides to every story. I don't know if I will ever know what really happened between them. I do think they were both doing the best they could.

My mom, sister Nancy and I went from living in a beautiful, large home to a smaller house on the south side of town. We went from great abundance to financial difficulties. Even though I always had what I needed, I knew we were struggling because Mom complained about money saying, "it doesn't grow on trees." I became fearful that there would never be enough of anything.

Mom got remarried. She met the love of her life, my stepfather, Charlie, and they wed when I was 10 years old. Charlie was a creative, passionate man who adored our family. He was of Arabic descent so I was fortunate to have an experience of non-white culture at a young age. Charlie restored a sense of family and filled our house with music and love.

The feeling of creativity in my family made it feel whole. There was celebration and purpose. Family members and friends came over to the house on holidays and random nights to play cards and eat cake. Mom always said that I had to have a well-rounded life to have a good future. Music and creativity were important to a vibrant existence. I learned this from Charlie.

There was a clunky electric organ in the corner of our living room. Charlie would sit there and sing at the top of his lungs, "Once in love with Amy, always in love with Amy!" and many other campy songs. I was fascinated with his ability to play by ear. He never had a music lesson in his life. I was fighting to win at trumpet playing, practicing every day. Mom used to say, "How do you get to Carnegie Hall, Amy? Practice, practice, practice."

Carnegie Hall was not in my future vision. I didn't know why it mattered and I had never been there. But it should be something I strived for.

Growing up always involved striving for something, reaching, pushing myself to do more, be more and feel something more.

I remember going to a Sunday church service with a girlfriend and feeling what I now call a spiritual hunger. I was envious that my friend's family had religion, even though the service was foreign to me and I didn't understand it. People seemed to be soothed by the religious service and I yearned for that feeling and understanding.

Mom and Charlie worked together at his carpet store, Township Carpet & Cleaning Co. on Jericho Turnpike. They sold cleaning services, wall-to-wall carpeting and oriental rugs. We called it "The Shop." My sister Nancy and I would go with Mom on a hot summer day and run around or play in the back. We would grab a carpet sample and go flying down the roller bars that moved huge rolls of carpet from the massive shelves to the delivery truck.

I remember being fascinated with the small, private office and wish I learned about running the business. I was so detached from the realities of life at that age.

There was a tile store next door. The lady who worked there drank 10 cans of Tab soda a day. Someone said she was going to get cancer from all that saccharin-sweetened soda.

Whenever we were at The Shop, Nancy and I would go to the convenience store a few doors down to get some candy. My favorite was Kit Kat because it reminded me of my best friend, Jody. Whenever Jody and I would get our hands on a Kit Kat, we would break off each of the four little bars and nibble off all the chocolate around each bar. Then we'd peel each thin layer of the crispy wafer from the top. We ate the candy like a tiny little mouse. It took a good 10 minutes to finish it. I have many snippets of memories like this from that time of my childhood.

We'd get coffees for Mom and Charlie. He drank his black and Mom took a splash of milk. The lid of the tiny Styrofoam cup would run over with coffee and I'd try not to spill it. Charlie would give Mom little gifts like small squares of Special Dark chocolate, or just try to make her laugh and smile with whatever he said. There was a sense of joy in our lives from the little things. I was safe. I had everything I needed and more. Charlie had put an extension on our house and created a huge living room and master bedroom. We had a large in-ground swimming pool in the back yard.

At 14, I had a summer wake-up ritual involving our pool. I set out my black one-piece terry cloth bathing suit on my bed right before I went to sleep. When I woke in the morning, I put the bathing suit on, making sure I didn't wake myself up too much. I stopped in the bathroom to pee quickly then quietly walked through the house, trying to keep myself half-asleep. I opened the sliding glass door. Once outside, I stepped to the edge of the pool. I took a deep breath, put my hands together above my head, slightly bent my knees and dove in. A RUSH, AWAKE! It was my favorite way to wake myself up in the morning. I performed this ritual over and over again that summer. Later in the morning, Charlie would come out to the pool and go for a dip. "Good Morning, Amy!" he'd smile at me with the biggest grin. He'd dive in too and swim lap after lap.

We had an electronic pool cleaner device that Nancy and I named Murphy. It looked like an octopus. Murphy was a round floating machine with long tentacles that blew out air and cleaned the pool. Sometimes one of the tentacles would brush up against me when I swam. It tickled my leg. Murphy was a machine personified. Sometimes I'd shout and laugh at him, "Hey Murphy, get out of my way!"

A couple times a month, on Sundays, we'd go to my Dad's house for the day. Either we stayed at his house, went fishing or to the movies. When I was 13, Dad took us out on a chartered fishing boat. There were 20 people on the boat plus the small crew, Dad, my sister and me. The air was chilly, breezy and salty. The sun shone brightly. We were bluefish fishing although many people were catching sea robins. "Some people like to eat them," Dad said.

The sea robins looked like birds. They were too beautiful to eat although some people said they were ugly. I went inside the cabin to escape the wind and think about what I could do to help those fish. It seemed like a good idea for me to wait for everyone to come inside then I would free the sea robins. Soon, the fishermen came in, celebrating their catches of day with drinks and laughing. While no one noticed, I snuck outside and grabbed the edge of the white plastic bucket full of sea robins. There had to be 15 or more crowded in there lying on top of each other. I grabbed the bucket and tipped it over the side of the boat and set them free into the ocean. I jumped up and down and clapped my hands, smiling for the triumph of freedom. Dad was really mad at me for that. So were the fishermen. "Amy, that was someone's food for the next week," he said. I cringed.

Part of me felt bad because they were mad but I felt justified. I didn't understand how my actions affected other people. I felt compassion for the sea robins stuck in a suffocating bucket. I don't remember if I got in any real trouble for my devious behavior. It wasn't my property to take or judgment to make. I still feel self-righteous about that decision. Those bird-like fishes were glad I did it.

On non-Dad weekends, I'd spend time with Charlie. He had a 1984 Z28. It was brand new, with t-tops, a beautiful grey exterior and a grey cloth interior. Mom said it was his mid-life crisis car. I loved to ride in it. Charlie and I would go to the local bakery and get a baker's dozen of assorted bagels. I am truly a New York bagel snob. Nowhere in the entire world makes them better than New York. Standing in the busy bakery on Sunday morning, full of people, one of the bakery girls would yell out the numbers from behind the counter.

One Sunday, we got there around 7:45 a.m. and there was a packed crowd. The bakery smelled warm, like cinnamon crumb coffee cake, the kind with the big crumbs cut in large squares.

"Number Eleven!" the girl in the white tee shirt and bakery hat shouted.

"Yes good morning," Charlie said. "Amy, tell them what we'd like dear."

I responded, "Hi, yes, may we please have two everything, four sesame, four onion, two cinnamon raisin and one plain." This was the perfect bag. We'd also get plain and veggie cream cheese, and a half a pound of smoked salmon. Sometimes we would get some of the coffee cake squares, but usually Auntie brought over Entenmann's when she'd visit.

After the bakery, Charlie and I would take a drive before heading home. I remember one particular Sunday we went to Republic Airport to look at the small planes. We got close and I posed for a picture. I pretended like the plane was mine, and I'd be hopping in to jet off to some secret location that hides celebrities.

I yearned to be an actor to escape the discomfort of being me. I auditioned for school plays and also studied musical theater at Usdan Summer Camp for the Arts. In high school, my teenage years were awkward and there were no leading roles for me. I was not one of the popular girls. My peers and I got along all right and I didn't get too much ridicule, but I never fit in with any of the cliques. My abilities just needed the opportunity to shine so I could succeed. I was a successful high school trumpet player, taking first chair from all the boys and the only trumpet-playing girl. That was not enough. For my acting pursuits, in 10th grade, I landed a role as Mae Peterson, the Jewish grandmother in *Bye Bye Birdie*. I nailed it and got my first standing ovation. I was at once satisfied. I also got drunk that night for the first time. That also filled me with satisfaction.

One of my sister's friends had a cast party and I got my hands on a bottle of Crème de Menthe. I drank half of it straight from the bottle while walking down Sleepy Hollow Road with the cast of the play. The liquor was thickly sweet, hot and fresh at the same time. It was disgusting and fabulous. That awkward feeling of not belonging washed away. I chugged the sweet elixir directly from the bottle. Walking in the dark, in a pack of kids. Laughing and feeling free, this was IT. My solution. I ran into the woods high as a kite and puked hard. My head was spinning. I felt like crap and fantastic at the same time. I finally understood what others had liked about partying. It took the edge off. I was still in the mindset of the good girl though. It would be years before my alcoholism would rise to the surface and command its takeover.

Mom discouraged me from pursuing a career in acting. She said I needed something to fall back on and I should consider business school. Even though Mom always told me I could do anything I wanted, I felt a need to be smart about it. I thought maybe I'd become an entertainment lawyer. I loved to be right and to win at anything. I figured I belonged hobnobbing with celebrities. Perhaps that would become my path. Law school would never find me. My ostentatious feelings of both superiority and inferiority were constantly at odds with each other. I reached for seemingly impossible goals then brushed them off when I attained them and went for the next opportunity. Stopping for a moment to feel the achievement and celebrate it — well, who had time for that?

I was at odds with my sister Nancy most of the time. We seemed to be so different and I wondered if we were even truly biologically related. She was tall and beautiful with long, brown hair and a square face. I was jealous that I didn't look like her at all. My red hair and freckled skin didn't allow me to get tan. Instead, I burned. Nancy was part of the high school clique that followed The Grateful Dead. She wore beautiful Indian skirts over her black, one-piece bathing suit.

Nancy knew how to put on makeup. She plucked her eyebrows and burned her black eyeliner with a lighter before she lined her lower lids with it. It baffled me that I didn't know how to do the things she did — I barely even felt like a girl. My awkward feelings left me separate and alone. Nancy seemed to have everything — friends, popularity and good times in her life. I was not happy. I was always judging her and often tried to do the opposite of whatever she did.

When I was 15 and in my uncomfortable, awkward youth, tragedy came to visit. Mom, Charlie, Nancy and I were out at Chi Chi's Mexican Restaurant for a family dinner. It was not somewhere we usually went to eat, but it was close to home. I loved the taste of salty Mexican food with its melted-cheese goodness. Charlie excused himself from the table and was in the bathroom for a while. He came back, muttered something to Mom and we abruptly left the restaurant. We hopped in the car and went straight home. I didn't know what was going on. I thought maybe the food made him sick.

Charlie went to the hospital that night. I think he drove himself there. I don't remember much about what happened. The next morning, I went to Usdan day camp where I was majoring in musical theater. Outside of the classroom, I waited for modern dance to begin and thought of Charlie.

An incredible wave of sadness overtook me. I felt a pain in my solar plexus and I began to cry. Somehow felt in my heart that Charlie had died. There were no cell phones back then to check in with anyone, so I didn't know what was going on with him. Was he okay? A feeling of deep, dark dread filled me to my core.

When I returned home that afternoon, I remember the large yellow school bus rattling up the street, my hands on the metal bars of the tall green vinyl seats, and my fear welling up inside. The bus turned up my street, and I leaned my face against the window to look toward my house. As we got closer, I saw more cars than usual out front. Mom was standing in the driveway waiting for me with her head in her hands. She was sobbing. I knew at that moment that my feeling earlier was correct. Charlie was dead.

It turns out that Charlie was bleeding internally from diverticulitis. Within 24 hours of going to the hospital, Charlie was gone and our world busted. Mom said that doctors let him bleed to death; she was utterly devastated. She went from being strict, not letting me go out with friends every weekend, to completely checking out of life and parenting. She wasn't able to be there for me as she couldn't be there for herself. The love of her life was gone. Mom's hair turned from auburn to stark white within three weeks. She stopped accepting calls from friends and family. She cut herself off from the world. I was alone at 15 years old.

I had some exposure to loss before this, but it was nothing like losing Charlie. My paternal grandfather died on the same day, August 17, the previous year. I don't remember his funeral but I do remember being deeply sad to have lost my grandpa.

My mother's parents died when I was four so I didn't have any memory of losing them. Charlie's mother had also died while he was in our lives. When she was in the hospital, we would go to visit her. Mom would drop off Nancy and me in a small and greasy hospital cafeteria for a couple of hours. I found it odd that no one else was in there but the line cook, Nancy and me. We would get hot chocolate and French fries. Sometimes we would order grilled cheese. The food was always comfort and distraction.

After Charlie died, my sister turned to her friends for support. I quit my extracurricular pursuits of drama club, Mathletes and trumpet playing in the jazz and marching bands. I stopped spending time with my well-behaved, smart and kooky friends. I remember feeling filled with shame at the death of my stepfather. I wanted to tell everyone and scream down my high school hallway, "Charlie died, you fucking assholes! I hurt so much. I want to die too!" But I stuffed those feelings deep inside my soul. The pain, sorrow, anger and confusion would sit there, like a deep-dark pit, empty and broken, at the bottom of my devastated soul. I didn't know how to process this death event. Instead, I started hanging out with friends who cut class and caused trouble.

My spiritual hunger increased as life went on. When Charlie died, I turned toward darkness and self-destructive choices to help me cope with life. I still had my good-girl mindset, but I was making decisions that would lead me, eventually, to become a daily drinker and the realization that I am an alcoholic. All of this brought me back to the spiritual hunger.

When I was 17, a senior in high school, I started drinking and smoking pot and cigarettes. My drinks were mostly Bartle's and James mixed-berry-flavored wine coolers and White Russians. I drank purely for effect. I could feel comfortable in my skin when I drank. Alcohol was a great confidence booster and comforter. I'd also experiment with other drugs when I had the chance. My friends and I tried acid, mushrooms, crystal meth and cocaine. Thank God I only dabbled and never got immersed and addicted to those other substances. Those drugs were scary. I knew deep down that playing with those powerful drugs was playing with fire.

I found a few friends I thought wouldn't desert me, as long as the liquor and the smoke flowed. I felt like I belonged somewhat and had an outlet for my pain. As long as I was high, I felt like a cool kid. But I wasn't. I was lured in by a desire to stuff my feelings and escape feeling badly. I had no tools to deal with my grief or shame surrounding the death of my stepfather, the abandonment by my mother and father or my feelings of isolation. The comfort of substances soothed me for a while.

My decisions were not well thought out and I was distracted. I got myself into college without much encouragement from anyone else. It seemed like the only thing to do. My schools of choice were both private and on Long Island: CW Post and Hofstra University. I applied and got accepted to both. For no apparent reason, CW Post became my school and I picked my major from a brochure because I liked the sound of "public relations." These choices were made without much thought or understanding. I would say I was lazy about it, but in retrospect, my grief was driving and I had no direction or help from others. My life was on autopilot and it was all I could do to try and make the right decisions.

My mother was supportive financially for nearly all of my undergraduate college tuition. I worked in a deli 30+ hours a week for my supplemental living expenses.

At age 18, I had a serious boyfriend for the first time. I met Daniel through a friend of my best friend in college at a party. Daniel and I partied together and were in young love. We became attached very quickly and were together for three years. I was staying at Daniel's house most nights, and his parents place in Centerport had become my second home.

One weekend, we went on a trip to upstate New York. Our friend Bill had a family home there. On the drive up, Daniel, his friend Bill and I were in Bill's truck, driving along backcountry roads for many miles. We came upon a bunch of cars and some young adults milling around in the woods.

"Hey man, look, a party!" Bill said. "Let's go!" Bill was single and always wanting to find girls. So we crashed the party. At one point, I said to Daniel, "I'm going back to the truck. I'll see you guys there." I was uncomfortable in this pack of a hundred strangers. I wasn't a huge fan of beer or keg parties. I chugged what was in the red solo cup and walked out in the street. I hung by the truck and lit a cigarette. I got this feeling like something was wrong. In the pit of my stomach, I could sense something unnamable. I heard a voice in my head, "get on the truck."

I jumped up on the back bumper. Seconds later, a car screeched around the corner, headed straight at me. The car crashed into the back bumper, right where I was standing. I was thrown from the back of the truck and flipped to the side of the road. I was screaming. Other people started running and screaming. Chaos ensued. Partygoers scattered everywhere. They were getting in their cars and driving off. A few people hovered over me and asked if I was okay. I wasn't. But I was conscious.

Before much time had passed, Bill scooped me up and put me in the truck. Daniel ran around trying to find out where the hospital was, frantically asking the inebriated kids where we needed to go. There were no cell phones or GPS devices in 1988. There were no houses nearby to borrow the phone and call an ambulance. We had to rely on people and directions. Bill drove me to the hospital about 20 minutes away.

I was in excruciating pain. My side hurt and my foot was completely swollen in my boot. I had broken my ribs and foot. Healing would take some time. I never felt safe in a car after that unless I am driving.

It turns out the driver was drunk that night — he drank a case of beer and got in his car moments before hitting me. My mother hired and attorney and sued him. We won $10,000 in the settlement and used it to pay for one semester of college.

The universe was trying to get my attention — maybe I should take a look at my drinking and partying? No, I'm not like that drunk guy that drove and hit me. Yet I was oblivious and continuously seeking oblivion. I was not spiritually awake, aware or able to honestly see myself. I was like that man as much as anyone else who drank like I did. I just couldn't see it.

The relationship with Daniel ended abruptly after he cheated on me with his sister's friend. At that point, my living situation shifted again. I toggled between my college best friend's house and my Mom's where there was a lot of tumultuous fighting going on while my Mom was at work. My sister, her husband, and their baby had moved in. There was household drama that I wanted to avoid. They were partying hard. My niece was just born and there was chaos and excessive noise. I couldn't be there and felt homeless.

Our family financial struggles continued. Mom asked me to co-sign a mortgage with my brother-in-law and I was not willing to do it. I backed out at the last minute and caused a huge riff in the family. I didn't want to be part of the drama that was happening at home.

My undergraduate degree was done. I earned a Bachelor of Fine Arts in Communication Arts with a specialization in public relations but I didn't feel like my education was complete. I took out a college loan. I moved from home to campus to pursue a Master of Business Arts degree in Marketing. This was perfect because I could avoid living at home and getting a full-time job.

I excelled in the MBA program, but hated it. I was motivated only by the idea of future financial success and stability. I was not living by heart, rather by potential gain. This approach has never worked well for me. When I choose financial over heart reasons, the universe responds with a resounding NO.

In my second semester of graduate school, I switched my major to English. I persuaded the Dean of Students three weeks into the semester that I had to transfer or I'd quit school. She let me get away with that.

I loved the Master's English program. I wrote a paper about the award-winning novelist Jerzy Kosinski. One day, I turned in my paper to the English professor. Later that day, a friend of mine who was friends with my teacher left a sticky note on my door: "Amy, Jerzy Kosinski is dead." I thought that meant I failed my paper and the professor hated it. This is the kind of thinking that got me into trouble and enticed me to drink. I didn't fail. I got a B+. At the time, I was paranoid. Kosinski died the day I turned in my paper. My friend's note was literal, not ominous. I thought that timing was a sign or clue that I was in alignment with universal energies. Synchronicity is not merely a coincidence.

During this time, I was co-writing a column for the college paper with a friend. It was a collaborative writing adventure on the Long Island nightclub scene. Specifically, we wrote about restaurants and local attractions. My co-writer, Shana, and I loved being wined and dined by restaurant and nightclub owners looking for free publicity and promotion. As a result, we built a name for ourselves in the local scene. Shana did most of the writing as she had a strong personality and conviction about how the articles should read. I convinced myself that Shana was a better writer than I — and she likely was. I didn't give myself the creative freedom to experience the craft. I was happy playing co-pilot, sharing the byline and going along for the ride. In between and during our writing gigs, school, and work, we partied, smoking pot and drinking whatever we wanted. We would hang out with other creative, artsy types and stoners. The party lifestyle was always running in the background. It became an ongoing theme for the next 20 years of my life. And I was completely oblivious to its existence, influence and control over me.

I had been working part-time in the university's public relations department writing press releases and media alerts. That position started as an unpaid internship that slowly moved to a part-time paid position. But I was impatient and I wanted real work. I didn't want to work and wait for a bigger opportunity. I quit. My part-time deli job was awkward even though the money and experience were good.

It felt as if I was wasting time. The Master of Arts in English was not going to do much for my life at that point. It would cost an additional $30,000 to complete my degree and I was bored with the curriculum. I was mostly reading books and writing papers about them. I could continue reading books on my own. It was time to do something that required my college degree. I dropped out of graduate school and quit writing with Shana.

Shortly thereafter, I made friends with a woman who was a singer and we connected with a guitar player. We started partying together and making music. We formed a threesome acoustic band we named *Beyond*. I was singing harmonies in a band, writing songs, and partying a lot. I had many adventures in that musical world for a year, including the time that Blondie lead singer Debbie Harry saw us perform in a tiny little bar in New York City's Lower East Side. This was the '90s. I wore combat boots, camouflage shorts and a black tank top. I drove my 1986 Firebird. My natural flaming red hair suited my wild personality. I thought I knew it all and I hadn't a clue. I was oblivious and seeking oblivion while trying to find a sense of a normal life.

Calling around to advertising agencies, I found employment as a receptionist. My job was to answer the phone, deliver faxes to their intended recipients and welcome people. This job was serious business. Answering the phones was important, as I was the first contact anyone had with this agency. "Good Morning, KZS Advertising," I'd gleefully say, then handle the call. I wondered if I really needed a college education to do this. It was my entry-level experience as a female employee in the advertising world.

The art director at the agency, Evelyn Rysdyk, asked me to type a paper for her as a side job for extra cash. It was about Shamanism. I had not heard of it before. I attended a regular women's drum circle Evelyn and her partner Allie held at their home and learned more about this modality. I participated in a weekend intensive in NYC with a notable shaman, Michael Harner, author of *The Way of The Shaman*. I learned to journey on the sound of a drumbeat. Shamans journeyed to alternate realities by meditating to the sound of a drum. I tried and practiced it. I met a spiritual teacher in the upper world and my power animals in the lower world. It was intense and fascinating. This was my not-so-subtle entry onto a spiritual path. A beginning.

My life was double sided. I was spiritually seeking and self-medicating. I was chasing everything outside of myself while looking for healing within. I was not healing I was escaping. When the working and partying lifestyle eventually fell apart, I met and fell in love with Jeremy, a man from Connecticut I met through a friend.

Chapter Two:
Synchronicity

"That which oppresses me, is it my soul trying
to come out in the open, or the soul of the world
knocking at my heart for its entrance?"
- Rabindranath Tagore

Synchronicity

Jeremy was tall and quirky like me. He had sandy blonde, curly hair and a big nose. He loved to get high and go on adventures. After we met in my friend Stacey's kitchen over bagels and lox, we became infatuated with each other. I'd work all day at the ad agency and drive my Firebird up to Connecticut. Jeremy and I would party and have sex. I'd spend the night, then leave at 4 am to go to work. Sometimes Jeremy came to Long Island, but mostly I escaped to Connecticut on weekends and several weeknights. It felt like freedom to speed up I-95 in my sports car, pushing 90 at times and feeling charmed that I didn't get pulled over. I did this side commute for four months until Jeremy asked me to move in with him.

I quit my Long Island life, the band and my agency job. I moved in with Jeremy without any work or a plan to create my new life.

My first job in Connecticut arrived with serendipity when I walked into the offices of the *Hartford Planet*. I had found a copy of the small, colorful magazine at the Middletown Chamber of Commerce. I believed in signs and thought that finding that magazine was the universe guiding me. I drove to Hartford's Bartholomew Avenue and found the office. It was a huge brick and cement building next door to the Spaghetti Warehouse. I went inside to find a hallway and reception window.

"Hi," the young woman receptionist named Kathy greeted me, "Are you here for the three o'clock interview?" "Yes," I smiled, "Yes, I am!"

The person scheduled for the job interview hadn't shown up. The magazine was looking for a writer covering the local music and entertainment scene. Hot damn! I had my articles and writing samples from my college paper in my portfolio, along with a few other sample articles I had written for a local Long Island newspaper. I had experience singing in the band and booking gigs in New York so I had a feel for the local music industry. They hired me on the spot. I asked to name my position and decided on Progressive Columnist. The job paid $17,000 a year, a drastic cut in pay from what I made as a receptionist at a Long Island ad agency. I figured it was the price I had to pay to work as a woman in a creative field. The extreme synchronicity of that moment was too sublime to ignore.

I held that position for 11 months. Management was spread too thin so employees frequently had to wait to receive our paychecks. We would sit around on Fridays and wait for the managing partner to show up. The office manager would tell us she couldn't give us our checks until he said so, and they had to make sure there was money in the account. I think that was illegal. I had no concept of what it was like to run a small business, so I figured it was just bad management. It was hard to live on a low salary and not know when funds would be available. I decided that even though I loved the work, the uncertainty of pay was emotionally upsetting. Shortly after I gave my notice, I landed a job in the advertising world once again.

My new job was with a small, successful, full-service advertising agency in Glastonbury, CT. The creative director hired me to be Group Coordinator for his team. This was a path to Account Executive. I was promoted from Coordinator, to Assistant Account Executive to Account Executive, which I attained swiftly in two and a half years. The entire time, I yearned to write. I wanted to be a copywriter. Jay, the creative director, told me: You are either account or creative, you can't be both. Once you are on one side, you can't jump over.

I was determined to prove him wrong. For four years, I worked at that agency and visualized my future writing job. The creativity within me was dying to be unleashed. I had no idea it was bubbling under the surface of my conscious life. I was too busy smoking pot and drinking to realize that I was stifling my inner artist.

Jeremy and I were married by then. Our life consisted of work and partying. I needed more of everything. Jeremy knew that I was determined to get a writer's job at Ames Department Stores, right up the street from where we lived. Anytime we drove by, I'd point and say, "I'm going to work there, Jeremy, as a writer." I said it for over a year.

One day, I saw an ad in the local paper for a copywriter position. That was my job. I was determined to get it. I sent my resume and cover letter and kept calling them, trying to worm my way in past Human Resources to the hiring manager. I didn't know much about corporations, so I just pushed and pushed until I got an interview. The hiring manager Deb told me it was my persistence that got me the interview.

Deb hired me as copywriter for Ames' annual toy catalog. I reviewed products, wrote snippets, ran the words by the legal and buyers departments and entered them into the layout. It was a cool gig. I loved that job. But people who hated their lives surrounded me.

Cubicle life was annoying. We were all on top of each other, separated by flimsy walls. I used to hear the lady next to me scraping her yogurt cup with a spoon. It was like nails on a chalkboard. I could measure the time of day based on the yogurt-cup scrape. I longed to shout over the cubicle wall, "Hey! I think you got it all!"

For a few years, I worked at Ames and got promoted to Manager of Advertising Services, which became more like an account manager position instead of a writer's position. I was back on the other side of things, weaving in and out of creativity in my work world. Eventually, Ames went out of business. My copywriter job ended and I returned to the advertising agency world as an account executive. It would be 15 years before the creative pull of writing would knock at my door again.

I was in the advertising industry for more than 20 years. It is a high-energy, dramatic career that chases you. If you are suited for the field and agency life, nothing else compares. Either you love it or you run screaming from it, unable to deal with the drama, clients and coworkers. If you've worked in this industry, you know what I mean. I have seen newcomers fall in love with the scene and thin-skinned, naïve people get crushed and leave.

My stints were in small-to-mid-size agencies. Later in my career, I tried working at a larger company. It was too corporate for my taste. By that time, I had become too much of an alcoholic to be a good employee.

The advertising world is a little like community theatre. There are individual and personal dramas within the overall drama of the company. I guess that is why I worked in both industries for a while. The drama and creativity fed me. When I meet people from advertising agencies, even to this day, I know they are in my tribe. The agencies where I worked varied in style but they all had a drinking culture in the forefront or background of client meetings, company gatherings or co-worker happy hours. Perhaps it is the nature of all society.

My daily pot smoking and weekend binge drinking distracted my creative energies further. However, the creative energy of the arts was always hovering and trying to sneak into my life. At that point, I was self-medicating my pain from the stresses of life in my 20s: unpaid bills, marriage problems, family issues and the pressure of an early career. There were no consequences for excessive wine drinking, daily pot smoking and occasional dabbling in other drugs so I was unaware that this was a problem. I thought I was spiritual and healing-focused because I sometimes took a yoga class and regularly read new age books. In reality, I truly didn't have the capability of being honest with myself.

Jeremy and I were struggling. The honeymoon stage of our relationship was long gone and our differences were emerging. He was living a fantasy world — always wanting to get high and escape. He was unsatisfied in his job of a copier technician and thought he shouldn't have to work at all. I was working full-time for an ad agency and felt resentful that he was always playing games on his computer or watching porn. I was disgusted more than I loved him.

As a creative distraction and something to do outside of work and home, I felt a soul gnawing to return to acting, one of my first creative loves. I have always loved the craft of acting. The experience of being someone else is thrilling to me. It's the opportunity to live countless lifetimes in one and take on many personas. I love the chameleon effect of becoming anyone at anytime. It feels like the utmost in creative expression as a human being.

When I'm going through a tumultuous time in life, I have come to rely on creativity to help me through. I get this tug from the inside that softly pulls at my creative heartstrings. The odd thing is that this pull can take me in many directions. Some artists focus on one genre. I do not. I have felt the call of many creative forms. Sometimes physical exercise and movement is my creative outlet. Sometimes it's visual art. Sometimes it's cooking. Sometimes it's making music. Acting is my longest love. It has always been my favorite. Creativity can be used for the pure joy of creation, to heal a hurt, or as a process to help get on the other side of hardship.

At the early stages of my marriage's emotional turmoil, I auditioned for various acting roles. I had to get out of myself and I was on a mission. I landed an ensemble part in *The Rocky Horror Picture Show* at The Little Theatre of New Britain. The following year, I got a leading role as Mary Bailey in *It's a Wonderful Life* at The Warner Theatre in Torrington.

On the set of Rocky, I met a dear friend, Ken, who became my best friend and a significant support person in my life during the decade that I transitioned from married to single to married again. More than 10 years later, that dear friend officiated my wedding to professional visual artist and love of my life, Tao LaBossiere.

I met Ken at rehearsal and we became fast friends. He adored me, and I him. The energy around our friendship was like the ones with my childhood best friends. We would get silly and laugh so hard. Ken had a cat named Oscar, nicknamed Scora D'Noir. This cat was hilarious and sweet. He'd startle easily. One time, we were hanging out at Ken's grandmother Rita's home in Farmington. There was a can of peanuts sitting on the kitchen counter. Rita shook the can hard for some reason, and Scora, sitting calmly on the floor, flung himself across the room with an unreasonable amount of depth and height. This spurred uproarious laughter from Ken and me. Scora developed an instant fear of the peanut can. We could shake it at any time, exclaiming "Peanuts!" at the top of our lungs, and laugh for what felt like eternity.

My relationship with Ken threatened Jeremy. Once on Jeremy's birthday, Ken unexpectedly landed in the hospital. Jeremy and I were assembling his new desk — one of those do-it-yourself pressboard kinds. My phone rang. It was Ken.

"Hey, Nish." he said.

"Hey, what's up? Why do you sound weird?" I said.

"I'm in the hospital, up at UConn. Can you come visit me?" he asked.

"Yeah, I'll be right over." I said. I looked at Jeremy, who was looking at me, furious.

"You've got to be fucking kidding me, Amy. It's my birthday and you're going to see him? What the fuck," Jeremy said.

"Are you kidding me?" I retorted. "My dear friend is in the hospital and you turn into a selfish asshole? I'm leaving." His rage at this uncontrollable matter was building. We were both pissed off.

"If you walk out that door, don't be surprised if we get a divorce." Jeremy said.

It was the first time the "d" word was ever mentioned in our relationship. That was a defining moment. From there, the decline of our marriage increased exponentially.

I was done. I couldn't wait to leave. I didn't want to be there with him to begin with. I had fallen out of love and I was quickly sliding into hate and resentment.

Ken was in the hospital for a few days and recovered fine. My relationship with Jeremy didn't fare so well. I started spending more and more time away from home to avoid being with him.

On most nights that year, I went to Ken's apartment in Hartford with the biggest bottle of high-end vodka the package store offered and a large bottle of diet Cranberry juice. We would get drunk slowly, chain-smoke cigarettes and sit out on his porch, chatting, screeching and laughing voraciously at the neighborhood stray cats that occasionally sauntered by. Our relationship was not only about laughing at cats.

Once, we saw a gang of neighborhood youth gather in the yard next door and start beating the living crap out of each other. The tension in the air was high. That honestly scared me. I was worried that a riot was going to break out. So I snuck to my car in the middle of the chaos and bolted from there to my home in Middletown.

I was usually pretty drunk by the time I was driving home unless I spent the night. My relationship with Ken was strictly platonic. He was 14 years younger than me, and while I loved him deeply, we never crossed a line beyond our intense friendship. I don't think I could have survived that time of my life without him in it. Life is pretty amazing to bring people, places and things in at the perfect time for the perfect lessons.

One night while leaving Ken's, I hopped on the highway going in the wrong direction. I was completely shitfaced and caught myself as I saw the cars coming at me. Thankfully, I panicked and quickly pulled off onto the wide shoulder. I took a breath and turned my vehicle around. My heart was pounding as loudly as my drunken head. It was a miracle I didn't get into a horrible accident or get arrested. I drove mindfully for the rest of the way home, even though I was quite drunk.

I drove intoxicated so many times, although I would not have admitted it and judged anyone else who did it and got caught. It was a large part of the denial of my alcoholism. I had no capacity for being honest with myself.

My first marriage continued to deteriorate. I was unfulfilled and resentful toward Jeremy and had no life tools to process the resentments. He cheated on me at a cast party while I was sleeping off a drunk and high stupor. What a real-life horror. The whole cast found out about it. I was mortified. He used the excuse that he thought I wanted an open relationship since we had a conversation about that once.

He was completely wrong. I could not get over that. His cheating was eventually the demise of our relationship. I was disgusted with him. I knew I could never be enough. He would always want more sex than I could give and he could never give me enough emotionally. We were at a stalemate. I was done. I would not forgive him to continue the relationship. I would check out emotionally as quickly as I could.

Chapter Three:
Crude Reality

♥

"All genuine art seeks the spirit."

- Rudolf Steiner

Crude Reality

Every relationship has an expiration date, whether it's from a one we create or one that's created for us. I could no longer be with Jeremy. There was too much damage done from his past indiscretions.

While some people might turn to an affair to distract the soul, I was searching for more actor opportunities online. I stumbled on a website for something called Oil Drum Art. I was not looking for visual art but somehow this popped up. I was intrigued by the concept of creating artwork on an oil drum and was inspired by the organization.

I instantly got a vision for a work of art involving an oil drum. I clicked on the contact page and wrote a message to the president of the organization, Jack Lardis. I found out later that Jack and I had mutual acquaintances in the advertising world. I requested a particular shape of oil drum to create my concept: a half oil drum cut vertically, with which I would create some visual art. Jack said yes, he just happened to have a drum, half cut, sitting in his warehouse. I made plans to go to Beacon Falls, CT to pick up the drum.

The work of art involved lots of magazine clippings of images and text. This first work of art creation consumed me. I was not thinking about my creative process. No one told me how to do it or what specifically to do. I just created what my mind visualized and kept going until it finished with me.

It took me three months. I had created my first mixed-media artwork, "Crude Reality". The creative experience of making visual art was cathartic, soul fulfilling and a good outlet for my sadness, rage and apprehension about the future. I needed healing in my life and art making provided it.

"Crude Reality"
by Amy LaBossiere
Photo: Ed DeGroat

Crude Reality made its first public appearance at the New Haven Festival of Arts & Ideas, on the city green. I loved seeing it displayed outside with the other artists' works. I couldn't believe it was happening. Accomplished, professional artists showed their work next to mine. I was having the time of my life.

Jeremy and I separated. In considering where I was going to move, I sketched a visual of what I wanted, including a several-floor apartment with an attached garage. I found an apartment matching my description in Farmington, CT, right on the Farmington River about 10 minutes from work. The space was a three-floor condominium apartment and I absolutely loved it. I took the cats, my couch, art supplies and clothing. I left Jeremy with most of our other shared belongings and his portion of the sale from our condo in Middletown.

It was an amicable divorce. Jeremy and I didn't fight over the separation of our stuff. Even when I hated him, I still loved him, and I knew our relationship's end was imminent. As long as I got the cats and my car, I didn't want any of the other mutual possessions. At the beginning of the end, the relationship spiraled down, mostly by the effect of my progressing alcohol problem (although I didn't know it at the time). The divorce happened quickly — in Connecticut there was a three-month waiting period and a hearing. Nothing was contested. I was relieved. I had no one to fight with or take care of. I felt free. Alone in Farmington, I could close my curtains at the end of my workday, pour a giant goblet of wine and create art.

The following year, I got a call from Jack Lardis, asking me to show Crude Reality in a Hartford gallery. I was excited to be in another Oil Drum Art show. Jack suggested I get a pedestal to display it and that I call the gallery director Tao to see if he had one. When I first spoke with Tao, he seemed irritated and distracted. He asked me to swing by the gallery and meet him.

Walking into the bright and airy gallery, I felt an attractive energy, like a buzzing in the air. There was Tao, walking toward me. He was handsome, in a fitted black t-shirt and paint-splattered jeans. His black hair was short and spiked. He had bright eyes and a sweet smile. Tao had an air of confidence and intensity about him. I was instantly attracted to him. He brought me to the basement to show me his storage space, and he pointed to a work area with paint and wood. "I can make you a pedestal," he said. "How tall do you want it?"

"You're going to make me a pedestal?" I said. "But you just met me, you don't even know me."

"That doesn't matter," he said. "You need one and I'm happy to do it."

Who does that, I thought to myself. Tao was a generous, sweet and gorgeous man. I wanted to know him more. We became fast friends. He helped me with my artwork, brought me art supplies and we started working together on the advisory board for Oil Drum Art a 501c3 organization. We attended New Haven Open Studios together. We spent time together drinking wine and conjuring up ideas for future art businesses. Our skills meshed well together. Tao is an extremely talented professional artist, and a great way of visioning the future. He sees endless creative possibilities and ideas. I know how to feed these abilities and visions. I have a marketing mind. We envisioned working together someday.

Once we took a trip to Still Waters, his family property. It was the most beautiful place I had ever seen. It had its own private pond and was where he grew up. Tao's mother lived in the main house. The four cottages and outbuildings were rundown but had so much potential. I loved it immediately.

Tao was in a long-term relationship with Angie but wasn't happy. I had started dating again but I wanted to be with Tao. I was in love with him. The guys I met never measured up to the bar Tao set. I tried some dating websites but never met anyone like him. I had to distance myself from Tao because it was too painful to be with someone that wasn't available. I sunk myself into my work. I got some acting and voiceover gigs and let life go on.

Meanwhile, I began my second major artwork. I had a fever for this art making as healing and expression thing. It was enjoyable and cathartic. I created "Legs," a life-size oil drum artwork covered in money from the top oil-consuming countries in the world. This work became the first conceptual piece I created.

My advertising influence was emerging. I remember the moment the concept came to me. I was on a flight with my boss from the ad agency, going to a new business pitch at a retirement community in the Midwest. I had my sketchbook and was jotting down visual ideas on what else I could create with an oil drum. I didn't know if I could get my hands on a smaller drum than the usual 55-gallon. I didn't know if such a drum existed, but it did. The 30-gallon drum.

"Legs" by Amy LaBossiere
Photo: Tao LaBossiere
In private collection.

My spirituality was simmering below the surface, pushed down and clouded by self-medication with alcohol and pot smoking. Mostly, I loved my Chardonnay. Luckily, I could hide my excessive overindulgence since it is socially acceptable to imbibe. Unless one is creating havoc and drama with DUIs and life issues, people don't question it. I continued. I created more artwork. I was also doing voiceover work while I worked full-time at the ad agency. And I was painting and sketching in between creating larger mixed-media works.

One night at a fundraiser at Real Art Ways in Hartford, I met Marty, a quirky and attractive architect. We started dating. Marty would text me at random to go out on dates. We had some fun times together.

He joined me on a work trip to Chicago and I tried to fall in love with him to distract me from missing Tao. Marty and I dated for six months until one weekend he randomly broke up with me.

We were driving out to Providence to go to *Waterfire*, a cool public art event on the city's rivers. Marty was emotionally distant and quiet as I drove. "Hey what's going on with you? Do you want to break up or something?" I half-jokingly said to him.

"Yeah," he said. "That's right."

"What the fuck, are you serious?" I said. "Are you fucking kidding me?"

"Whatever, yeah," he said. I never had someone break up with me and didn't really know why it was happening or how we got to that point. For Marty, the relationship was more casual than it was for me. I was distraught by it.

I called Tao — we hadn't talked in almost a year. He was upset when he picked up the phone. Angie had ended their relationship that weekend and was moving out. This was amazing synchronicity. We each got through the pain of our transitions and started dating. Things were somewhat casual at first. After a couple of months, he asked me to be his girlfriend. We picked up where we left off the year before and fell quickly in love.

We had many art nights fueled by wine and lovemaking. We were passionate about each other and our lives. We had our own interests yet completely adored each other. I finally understood what my Mom and Charlie shared. I understood what real love looked like.

Meanwhile, I became an amateur wine connoisseur. I would fill a shopping cart full of wine at the liquor store, a different store every week, like I was shopping for a party. Life was a continuous celebration. We attended art receptions, hosted parties, went to friends' houses. We drank and drank some more. Work was a bridge between drinking events.

My creativity was a response to my inner life. My artwork sometimes included dolls and Barbie® doll parts and images. As an adult, I used them to work through feelings of the impermanence of beauty and youth alongside unrealistic expectations of perfectionism. Healing through creativity is channeling all the power of the universe into a creative project. This can be done to heal others. Art as prayer is a possibility.

Once, my niece's boyfriend Joey was ill and in the hospital for kidney stones. Nancy called me one day and said, "It's horrible. Joey is in so much pain. Please pray for him."

I'm not sure why but in the moment, I decided to create a painting of him as a prayer. This prayer was a visual message to the universe asking for help.

I found a large piece of art paper and paint. I started by thinking of his face, visualizing him in my sensory field. I imagined him with all of his spirit guides and good energy beings surrounding and healing him. I painted what I saw in my mind's eye.

"Joey with Kidney Stones Healed"
by Amy LaBossiere

As any unseasoned artist might expect, I didn't create this image exactly as I saw it in my mind. It was my hands' interpretation of that picture, due to my artistic limitations. I am not classically trained but have allowed myself to create anyway.

Creating artwork requires forgiveness. I had to forgive myself for the inability to create what I saw in my mind. I wanted the advanced skill set of Tao, or another one of the talented artists in the world, to be able to create what I envisioned. But this is not the amateur's role.

Creating art is letting go.

Can I accept all that is, with all of its seeming imperfection, and realize it is an imperfect expression of creativity, healing, and love? This is why I create artwork. I create artwork in any form to allow its energy to come through me, as a soul manifestation with a purpose.

Chapter Four:
Thoroughly Unprepared

"Thoroughly unprepared, we take the step into the afternoon of life. Worse still, we take this step with the false presupposition that our truths and our ideals will serve us as hitherto. But we cannot live the afternoon of life according to the program of life's morning, for what was great in the morning will be little at evening and what in the morning was true, at evening will have become a lie."

- Carl Gustav Jung

Thoroughly Unprepared

Most of life is about being unprepared. Life is what happens when we're busy making other plans. Expect the unexpected. Just do it. Everywhere we are flooded with messages to remind us that we are unprepared for anything can happen. It can be unsettling or calming, depending on one's perspective.

As a spiritual person in a physical body, I strive for balance. I can see the positive and the negative in the concept of being thoroughly unprepared. Positively, I can trust that the universe will provide me with the tools and capabilities to handle anything. I can handle what's presented to me. The negative says, watch out, here comes life. Either way, I am thoroughly unprepared.

If I change perspectives to shift just a bit, this unpreparedness becomes openness: I can be open to change, new beginnings, possibilities and the opportunity to recreate myself every day, or as needed. I am open to evolving to my further potential. I am open to learning what I do not know or understand. The moment something is learned, I change. That is the physics of being in the moment and unraveling the mystery of life.

In the late morning of my life, I awoke to the notion that I am an artist. It was a profound awakening because most of my life I felt I didn't measure up. I didn't easily fit into any of society's molds or have an awareness of who I was. My life seemed less than charmed in my childhood. I now understand it is always charmed — I manifest what I need at the precise moment that I need it.

The "I" that I am referring to is the spirit I, the higher self I, the universal observed "I," not my ego. With this understanding of self-manifestation as an artist, I realize that my artist life was without the artist label. Now I have it. Others validate me while I create, submit, show and reveal.

My job at the ad agency didn't fit me anymore. I quit and moved in with Tao. We got engaged. I was ready to be an actor and artist. I'd give it a go. I landed a gig in Brooklyn, NY as a background actor for the indie film, *Adam.* The shooting day was 16 hours long and I made $58, barely enough for gas and tolls. This was very different from my $75,000 agency salary. Surely this wasn't sustainable.

I had to do something else. After a few months working freelance for a local ad agency, I found myself in the running for a full-time job at a larger, more corporate agency in Simsbury, CT. It was a large, well-established firm with a solid reputation. I got the job.

I'd drag myself out of bed at 6:00 am to get to there by 8:30 am. I liked to be early but that usually went unnoticed. I'd work all day, then feel guilty when I wanted to leave right at 5:30 pm. It was the end of the workday, yet so many employees stayed later. It was like they wanted to be there. Even if I waited an extra 15 minutes before I left, I'd feel like a total slacker. Walking through the agency halls, down the stairs and past reception, I'd see everyone plugging away at their desks, in meetings with others or on the phone. I did not want to be there. I wanted to be with Tao, living an artist's life. I had become a miserable clock-watcher and someone who lived for the weekend. It was not working for me.

After a few months, it was clear I didn't fit into that agency environment. I was struggling and back in a cubicle once again. After six months employment, I got my first bad job review ever. I was failing and unhappy. I wasn't sure how this was going to play out. I was drinking a lot, every night. Most work events included alcohol, so I could hide my issues in the social atmosphere of conviviality. But I was miserable.

I was spiraling, and the drinking was affecting my relationship with Tao. While under the influence of too much wine, I would get jealous of Tao's past relationships and question his love for me. We would have the same fight over and over again, when I found a photograph or painting of an ex-girlfriend, or one of her artworks that he saved.

"I'm your second choice," I'd slur at him unexpectedly, catching him off-guard.

"What are you talking about, Amy?" he'd respond.

"You only want to be with me because you can't be with her," I rationalized and spit anger, half screaming and half crying.

"No, that is a complete lie. You're an asshole!" He defended.

I was wallowing in issues that I didn't understand, fueled by too much wine and insecurity. I didn't know how to deal with this aspect of my personality. My fear of abandonment was running the show and making an unreal situation the track of my relationship. We always made up quickly and lovingly, but our arguments were heated and ugly.

Tao and I started seeing a couples' therapist named Peter to deal with what he called our "power struggles." Peter based his practice on the book *Getting the Love You Want: A Guide for Couples* by Harville Hendrix. The work helped me see how I brought my inner wounded child into my primary relationship with Tao.

I created a small sculpture in reflection of that time, "Getting the Love You Want." The piece reflected the dance of relationships and how people can hold an image of another in their hearts while in a relationship with someone else. I thought about my time with Marty when I wished he was Tao. I thought Tao wanted to be with his ex-girlfriend. I didn't realize that Tao chose me.

"Getting The Love You Want" by Amy LaBossiere

My next significant artwork was a large, 5-ft. tall acrylic cylinder I filled to the brim with wine corks. I sourced the corks from my stash over the years. I had an extra-large trash bag full of them. The rest came from friends and a local vineyard. The artwork had mannequin arms and blazing red hair coming out of the top. I called it

"Self Portrait: I can stop anytime I want." My blatant cry for help with this artwork was unconscious to me at the time, but not to others.

The work was on exhibit for Open Studio Weekend at Hartford ArtSpace Gallery. We volunteered to run the gallery in the apartment building where Tao lived. I was at the opening reception, dressed up and fully sauced by early evening. I was sipping the free Chardonnay from a 5 ounce plastic cup and was several cups in.

"I can stop anytime I want" by Amy LaBossiere
Photo: Tao LaBossiere.
In private collection.

Emily, the wife of an artist friend, approached me. She looked me up and down, looked at my artwork, and then said, "Amy, do you think you have a problem with alcohol?"

I laughed and said, "What?" I shuddered. "No, this is pure whimsy."

I was almost offended but thought it was a little funny. Emily continued, " If you ever want help, let me know."

She offered to bring me to a 12-step meeting. I laughed with my Chardonnay buzz on. I was a little pissed off about it. I wondered for a moment if she was right then I brushed it off. I had things under control.

Emily had planted a seed that would burst six months later — and again years later.

It was two decades after college and I returned to graduate school. This time, it was for a soul purpose. I was internally called to pursue a Master of Arts in Conscious Evolution, a 22-month program studying human consciousness.

Sometimes people ask how I came to study Conscious Evolution, and why. An excellent spiritual practitioner in my area, Robin Clare, sent out regular email blasts offering her services and other programs. The Graduate Institute (TGI) was mentioned in one of her emails.

It is similar to other "found activities" that work their way to me. It has happened in the acting world, the art world, the advertising and marketing worlds and anything in which I've ever participated. People, events and experiences have found me directly and indirectly in precisely the perfect moment. In cosmic synchronicity, it all comes together seamlessly.

Seeing the words Conscious Evolution and Master's degree together enticed me. I went to a TGI introductory meeting because I was pulled to discover it. I applied to the program, even though I didn't know it was perfect for me.

I didn't know how much the educational journey would improve my life, inspire change and create new pathways for how I engage with our beloved world. I didn't know about the fantastic people I would meet, like Ervin Laszlo, Rupert Sheldrake, Andrew Harvey, and many others that had a profound impact on me.

In my vision, I was thoroughly unprepared. But the universe will step up if I agree to look, listen and learn. While I was clouding my perception on a nightly basis, a bigger purpose was trying to get my attention.

I applied to the Conscious Evolution with the openness that is part of me — my desire to learn and grow. I trusted that this was part of the roadmap of my life. My higher self was driving and I was the conscious observer. But just like the rest of us, I was thoroughly unprepared. That was my plan with the Conscious Evolution Master's degree program. I was not sure what I was going to learn, but I knew I must participate. I was spiritually and intellectually compelled.

Sometimes people asked what I would do with that degree. What kind of job is that for? I didn't have an answer. Spiritual gangster? The best version of myself?

Frankly, it prepared me for nothing and everything at the same time. I was working in the advertising industry, quite unhappy with my job and myself. I was drinking way too much wine at night to self-medicate and get through the day. My soul was crying out, but I could not hear it.

I was accepted to the program and gleefully created my life to fit it.

The first change I made was to quit the full-time agency job. I had only been there 11 months, but it was draining me on so many levels. It did not fit who I was to sit in a cubicle all day long, five days a week in a toxic situation. It did not fit my relationship with a partner who makes his own schedule for me to be trapped in an inflexible work position.

The job also did not give me the time or availability to pursue the Conscious Evolution program. My soul saw this inflexibility as a metaphor for my life. I could not evolve and continue in the work I was doing. I had to find a source of income that could support my personal transformation and lifestyle I knew I wanted.

I called Mark O'Brien, the principal at O'Brien Communications Group (OCG). Mark was my supervisor at a previous agency and I adored him. He was thoughtful, a great writer and a friend to me in the business world. We knew each other for over a decade at that point. We had chatted for years about me going to work for him someday after he set out on his own. When I got accepted into the Master's program, I asked him to hire me. I called him from my car on my lunch break one day. "Hey Mark." I said.

"Hi Amy, it's great to hear from you. How's everything?" Mark said.

"Well, good and bad. I got accepted into a wonderful Master's program," I said, "But my job sucks. Actually, I think it's more that I suck at my job."

"A seed doesn't grow in sand, Amy," Mark said to me.

"What?" I said, confused by his comment. "What do you mean?"

"You are smart and a great marketing person. You were always a wonderful employee," Mark replied. "It's not the right place for you if it's not a good experience. A seed doesn't grow in sand. We need to get you out of there. Come work for me. How much do you want to make and how much do you want to work?" He asked.

Just like that, my life changed. We set up an agreeable, fair contract. I gave my notice to the old company, and felt so free. The agency respected and celebrated my choice for leaving. I was going to work as a part-time marketing strategist for OCG, pursue my Master's degree and begin life as some kind of artist. Eventually, I wanted to work with Tao on his business of murals and fine art commissions.

It was scary but I knew at my core that it was a soul imperative. A new life was calling.

Up to that point, I was drinking wine every night, barely exercising and taking antidepressants to keep me from smoking cigarettes. My art making progress had slowed while my alcoholism escalated.

Chapter Five:
Creative Process

♥

"To give birth to the unknown, we must be willing to step out of the way and take what comes, no matter how unacceptable it seems. Our deeper needs are not often served by following what we think we want or what makes sense. There is an intelligence behind the seeming random nature of our spontaneous images and forms. It deserves our trust."
- Michelle Cassou and Stewart Cubley,
Life, Paint, and Passion

Creative Process

At the end of the agency job and the beginning of my new life in graduate school, I needed a new creative outlet. I wanted to explore process painting. It focuses on the spontaneous activity of painting, not the end result of an imagined image. The artist takes a brush and intuitively selects the "correct" color. The brush is placed on the canvas and the work begins. The artwork begins to emerge out of its own creation. The artist is not supposed to judge what is being created, just let it flow.

Many artists contemplate an end result when they create. The landscape painter sees the landscape. A portrait painter sees the person. A photographer sees the image. The sculptor has a preliminary scale model of the final product, called a maquette. Even an abstract painter maps out her canvas with painstaking care. Many artists work backwards from the result. However there is another way of doing things. It is working in the process, in the moment, with no completed work in mind.

This process of art making can be difficult for artists, because it is intimidating to create without knowing what's coming out. What if it is ugly? What if it's no good? As an outsider artist, I found it exhilarating to create in a non-judgmental way. Because I had no formal art training, unlike the many trained artists in my sphere of influence, I would often feel intimidated or inadequate of my painting abilities. I was not trained or practiced in the genre.

We had an arrogant neighbor at ArtSpace that was always judging others' work in this way. "It's so amateurish," Greg would often criticize other artist's work and say, "That work is shit. I can't believe he sold even one."

This kind of comment made me shudder. Why should anyone be shutting down anyone's creativity? I think Greg had issues with his own artistic abilities and inadequacies. It reminds me of what we say about guys that drive huge, obnoxious trucks. What are they over-compensating for?

I signed up for a four-week workshop with my friend Roberta Mockus, an award-winning process painter and professional artist. Tao and I recruited our friend and neighbor, Jim, to join us. We were all looking to do something creative and have fun. The first night of the workshop was the same day that I acquired books for my graduate program, one that was on process painting. The timing seemed auspicious.

We drove up to South Windsor. Roberta greeted us at the door and led us to her studio basement. It was an unfinished laundry room with easels and paints everywhere. There were a few other students already set up. I picked a spot behind one of the basement support beams to create my first process painting. Roberta was standing there, clutching a book as she spoke to us. I looked more closely. It was one of the books I had just bought earlier that afternoon, *Life, Paint & Passion*. I found out that Roberta had studied with the authors, Michele Cassou and Stewart Cubley. They were her mentors and this workshop was based on their teachings.

My art-making process was already based on intuition, impulsive energy and vision. Process painting pushed the boundaries of my creation to a spontaneous source. It encouraged me to think with a child-like mind and allow whatever came up to manifest and be painted on the canvas. Since I am what is called "an outsider artist" with minimal training, I found it rather easy to let go.

Classically trained artists sometimes have a difficult time with process painting. They have to ignore or set aside their education. They have to re-learn how to let creativity flow.

When a work of art is created, it has a life force of its own. It has a consciousness that arises with an aliveness that is similar to being born. With process painting, I remembered what it was like to be a child, painting with my fingers, creating for no reason, out of my imagination, with nothing to do but be in the moment.

Process painting allows the artwork to flow through the artist as if it were a birthing experience. This can happen for any person that will allow it. Artists will find that they break through any pre-conceived notion of who they thought they were, and non-artists will find that they have creativity waiting to arise from within.

The purpose of painting in this spontaneous way is to free us from the tightly woven shells of our self-knowledge, not to create more limiting labels, more definitions about ourselves. On the contrary, we already know too much about ourselves. Perhaps we need to unlearn what we think we already know. Perhaps we can let go, and outgrow our own limitations.

Creativity can be used as a tool to find the inner voice. If I listen quietly, I will hear the sounds of inspiration.

Roberta started the session with a guided meditation. She said, "Close your eyes. Take a few deep breaths. Now think about what you want to heal within yourself. Listen quietly for any guidance."

During the meditation, I heard the word "acceptance" in my mind's ear, and saw a vision of wishbones in my mind's eye. I could feel that this image was about healing my family dynamic. I had family issues to heal, and those issues were attempting to emerge.

The process painting experience triggered further insight and meditation. After the painting session, I meditated. I asked the art questions, then waited for the answers:

• What part of me needed healing?
• What were the colors telling me?
• What could restore peace and harmony to my life?
• What did I need to learn about myself?

Eventually, I threw that painting in a dumpster. Sometimes I don't want to look anymore.

We have to push past the inner critic when creating and listen for it deeply, beyond the ego. It will give us valuable suggestions. Not the ones that want us to buy things or tell us continuously about all our flaws and shortcomings, but the ones that subtly introduce change and conscious evolution. With these suggestions, the artist finds creativity and inspiration. From that creativity arises authentic self-knowledge and self-awareness with room to grow.

Creating artwork in the process format leads to an awareness and self-knowledge that is beyond my thinking mind. I create as if I am a child, without judgment of what I am doing.

It is not about creating beautiful art, although a work of fine art may be the final result. The purpose here is to navigate our inner world and listen to the voice within. If we experience a feeling of blocked creativity, it's because we fear the learning and awareness that is waiting to reveal itself.

Making art can also heal. In a previous chapter, I mentioned the healing painting I worked on for the man who suffered from kidney stones and went to the hospital for surgery. This painting was not for public display or fine art. It was a spiritual act — a prayer painting used to bring attention from the universe to transport the healing vibration to the subject.

So now I want to know why I create, and go deeper in search of the source. It feels like searching for the source of creation itself.

My experience of art making is directly related to my epistemology. Therefore, my creativity arises from spirituality and my connection to the divine. I feel the urge to create from a teleological perspective, meaning that it occurs from within and pulls me toward creation.

Chapter Six:
Conscious Evolution: Going Deeper

♥

"So many people don't know how to inspire
themselves. Use everything that moves you: music,
walking by water, flowers, photographs of the
enlightened ones. Inspiration helps so deeply in
overcoming laziness; summons what the Sufis call
the fragrance of the Beloved into everything."

- Andrew Harvey

Conscious Evolution: Going Deeper

At the first session of the Conscious Evolution cohort, on the Spring Equinox, I heard about learning as a biological imperative. It means that in our essence, humans are designed to want to learn. It was exciting to discover that at this moment change was entirely possible. Stasis was not necessary. I was encouraged to go on a new journey of inquiry and find my passion.

Including our program coordinator Charles, there were eight people in my cohort: Jason, the other Amy, Susan, David, June and Carol. We were together for 22 months. Half were teachers. For them, getting a Master's degree meant that they would get a higher paycheck and fulfill a work requirement. A few of us, including me, were working professionals. TGI called us colleagues instead of students because learning is interactive, not one-sided.

By the time the sessions began, I had left the full-time advertising job, and I was working part-time as a marketing consultant, living in an artist community, volunteering to co-direct Hartford ArtSpace Gallery and pursuing this degree.

We jumped in right away and were encouraged to work at the edges of our belief systems. We discussed how we don't *resolve* conflict. We *transform* it. We talked about how creativity is as important as literacy. We learned that if we were not prepared to be wrong, we would never create something original.

During our time together, our cohort pondered questions like this:
• How different would you be in a different context of existence?
• How much of who you are is really up to you?
• What is the full impact of your actions?

A marvelous and synchronistic aspect of this pursuit was that it inspired me to make art. This was not an arts-related degree. However, the content could not avoid the topic of art, because art and human consciousness are shown to progress and change on the same trajectory.

In other words, when humanity evolves, the contemporary artwork of that time also changes and advances. I decided in the very first session that art making would be an integral part of this experience.

So much of my own life was fraught with denial. I had trouble seeing myself, much like how a mirror and a photograph of oneself are different. We cannot see the truth of ourselves from the outside in. It needs to come from the inside. That is one of the reasons many people turn to different spiritual practices. They are looking for a way in from the outside.

There are many paths to get there. It can cause extra pain if you do this kind of work without cleaning out the garbage of the ego first. I spent a lot of time seeking before I did any internal housecleaning. Not that the time was wasted, but a layer of ick was in the way. That layer was killing me.

I found that the most acceptable, calming way to soothe my spirit was to drink wine: glass after glass, bottle after bottle. When it became an obvious problem, I tried to ease up on my own a few times. I attempted control with my fierce willpower, then by wishing it, or stating positive affirmations. I thought maybe drinking more water would help. There was the glass of wine, glass of water rotation. I got many cases of the fuck-its as I tried to gain control. I tried changing drinks. I tried taking days off. I was mentally obsessed and wondered, "Hey, is this really a problem?"

I heard others say: "If you think you have a drinking problem, you probably do."

I hated that statement. I rationalized my drinking. It was just wine; how bad can it be? Everybody does it. *They* drink so much more than me. I don't drink every day (I did). I haven't lost *everything*. I haven't really lost *anything*, so what the hell. I can keep on keeping on. This kind of rationale is self-destructive, egotistical and avoiding. We have to face our troubles and fears. We cannot escape the hard work of conscious evolution if we want to grow spiritually and personally. For each of us, it looks different.

My personal inquiry and change began with the creation of artwork and intellectual exploration. I wanted to understand on a deeper level why I create and have creative desire. I also wanted to know why it took 35 years for me to unleash my inner artist.

When I reflect on the past, I spent twenty years avoiding the sudden, tragic death of my stepfather and childhood traumas. My creativity could not find ways to rise to the surface until I started to spiritually crack open.

A visionary art approach has been the crux of my personal transformation. The more I created, the deeper I got into myself. At the onset of the Conscious Evolution program, I made a personal commitment to create one work of art after each cohort weekend. These works were reflection artworks, created from a meditation on the weekend.

In my artistic exploration, I often brainstorm concepts and ideas for new art pieces. Usually, I had to wait for an idea to manifest within my mind when it was ready to be created. I wanted to examine the ways in which reflection art can be created. Then I could sit with the work, allowing it to present a deeper message.

On my way home from the first session, I had a powerful desire to paint. It is unusual for me because I am not a painter by artistic nature. Besides occasional process painting, I work mostly in mixed media and gluing things together. I was known in local art circles as a "glueist."

I imagined myself painting as I drove on the Merritt Parkway toward Hartford. I wanted to feel color on a huge canvas. I visualized sky-like blues and bright orange. I desired to slather paint on a canvas as if it were a wall.

Later that evening, I settled down, ready to get to the task. I searched the studio for a canvas. I found a smaller canvas than what I conjured in my mind's eye. A 10"x10" canvas would be my playground. I previously thought my medium would be oil paint, but now in the context of this smaller creation, I thought pastels and charcoal served my initiatives better. I put on some indie instrumental music and opened my journal to the day's notes. I searched for phrases and concepts that attracted me during the sessions to create a soul-portrait of myself in the experience.

This work launched my journey into Conscious Evolution and I created my first body of work. The images on the pages that follow are the springboard of that process that took place throughout the program.

In December that year, I got sober for the first time. It was the middle of winter. I was tired because Tao and I were drinking a lot of wine. At times, we'd both be in a blackout and have our sporadic and terrible screaming matches. It baffled me that we could love each other so much and fight like we despised one another. On any given night, our simple evening of drinking and watching Netflix escalated into fits of intense anger.

"Fuck you," I screamed at him, with my drunk and sloppy slurred words. He retorted back in defense. "Fuck you. You are a crazy asshole!" We were fighting about nothing in particular or noteworthy. We were drunk and off the rails. We recovered quickly after each argument. The lingering hangover still took its emotional toll.

One Saturday, our cohort took a trip to the Metropolitan Museum of Art. While at the museum, a painting by Jacques-Louis David, *Death of Socrates*, caught my eye. It captivated me so much that when I got home, I found the image online and stared at it. I wanted to create artwork inspired by that painting.

"The Death of Socrates"
by Jacques-Louis David
Metropolitan Museum of Art,
New York, Catharine Lorillard
Wolfe Collection, Wolfe Fund, 1931

I recalled reading *Passion of the Western Mind* by Richard Tarnas in May and learning about Socrates sentenced to death by drinking hemlock, seemingly by choice. He was ready to die. I thought about the image and story. It was an excellent metaphor for transformation. We change because we are ready for old parts of us to die.

Tao was having his own struggles with drinking. He decided to go to a 12-step meeting. While he was gone, I figured I'd have time to run down to Hot Tomato's and have a couple of glasses of wine. He left and returned about 20 minutes later. "What happened?" I asked.

"There was no meeting, so I stopped at the package store," Tao said. He pulled out a magnum of Chardonnay from the black plastic bag he held in his hand. We stayed up a few hours, drinking it until it was empty. The night was uneventful, but I woke up feeling like shit.

After considering more drinks the following evening, we talked it over and went to a 12-step meeting together instead. I decided to try to get sober. I went through a transformation by surrendering my addiction to alcohol. I would no longer consume wine. I had allowed a death to occur, completely by choice. That part of my existence seemed like it was ready to die.

I was surprised to find that the meeting was not what I thought it would be. I wondered where the derelicts were, and why everyone was dressed nicely. People were not drunk and creepy. Balanced diversity of race, gender, apparent socioeconomic backgrounds and lifestyles all came together to deal with a common peril, the troublesome issue of alcoholism. I wasn't thinking any of that when I walked in that fearful, dark first night. I've come to learn it over time.

Growing up, I thought an alcoholic was someone in a trench coat living under a bridge. I thought they weren't responsible, active members of society. They were bums as my grandma used to say.

When I was a kid, I remember seeing a public service announcement on TV. There was a single man, slumped in a chair in a stark room. A chilled male voiceover flatly stated, "If you or a loved one has a problem with alcohol, there is help. Alcoholics Anonymous." That shit was daunting. And I was completely wrong.

Most alcoholics have amazing willpower, intelligence and personal drive. They are smart, creative, funny and engaging. Alcohol was their solution in life to take the edge off of human existence until it didn't work any more, turned on them and became their obsessive ruler. It was also true for me.

My first meeting had a speaker named Peter. He was engaging and dynamic. He wore a red sweater and dress slacks. He was tall and handsome, with silver hair and sophisticated energy. He told his story with candor and humility. Peter talked about his corporate life and what it was like to become obsessed with alcohol while trying to run a company and a family. Both his professional and personal life unraveled from his drinking. At one point, Peter told us, he couldn't take it anymore, and sought help. Luckily for him (and all of us), there were meetings like this.

I sat there a bit dumbfounded — I had thought one thing and was experiencing another. This was good. I felt better in the moment. I wanted a bottle of wine that night, and for an hour or so, that feeling was held at bay.

A basket was passed around and people were pitching dollars in. I thought that was payment for Peter. It wasn't. It was for that meeting's general expenses like rent to the hosting facility and refreshments.

It was a Wednesday night, like any other evening. Peter shared his story and people in the group shared afterward. Each person who shared said something relatable about their drinking. I realized I might have a problem with alcohol. Perhaps there was a way I could deal with it, even though I didn't really want to. I sat and cried, although I didn't let anyone see that. My air of confidence blocked them from seeing my truth.

The art making continued throughout the two years of Conscious Evolution, until my artwork was shown at my first one-woman exhibit, *Conscious Evolution: Reflections on a Master's Program*, at Hartford ArtSpace Gallery.

I wrote corresponding meditations for each of the works of art. They were created as a path of inquiry and self-reflection to consider art for healing. The work will gladly meet you where you are, whether or not you already meditate. It does not require you to sit on a cushion for hours or do anything but read and think about the images and words. If you wish, you can let go of whatever you might be holding onto.

The practice of refining oneself is about softening our hard edges. It's about going within, looking around and seeing what's there.

To see full color versions of the following artwork and meditations, visit amylabossiere.com and click on *Conscious Evolution: Going Deeper.*

Square One

Beneath the calm exterior
is a fast-running river,
Flowing quickly as you
merge with life's tasks.

Take a moment
each day to integrate
your being with your essence
and the divinity within.

Fibonacci Chakra Curve

Stop looking at flaws to
distract you from your purpose.
Feel the way of the warrior,
of your true animalistic nature.

Be the love.
Grow like a tree.
Mature yourself.

River of Consciousness

Come let me show you the beauty of this world.

Everything is beautiful.

Your pain is beautiful.

Everyone is your teacher.

Everyone is your mirror.

Be here now.

In Keeping

The basis of human life
is to explore your boundaries
and finish your thoughts.

Focus your intention
and set to your task.

Ground yourself in a new
reality of your own making.

Blank Slate

The wheel of life is going to turn

whether you struggle or surrender.

Time is precious.

Your life is short upon this earth.

Shimmer in your existence.

Open your eyes.

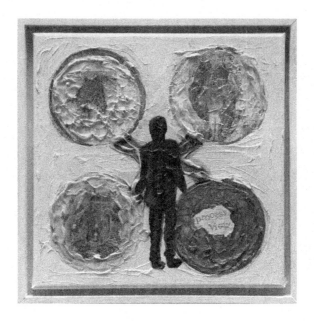

Process and View

Empty yourself of the training
you received up until now.
Abandon it, because now that you know how to live,
you need to learn how to die.
Separate from your body while you are alive,
so you can more easily transition later.

Morphic Resonance

Better that you be open to the impossible,

than restrict your soul

with the limits of possibility.

Communicate from the heart

and move there from your brain-mind.

Live in that place,

but don't forget to

occasionally visit the mind.

There is wisdom there.

The Akashic Field

Empty yourself of the training
you received up until now.
Abandon it, because now that
you know how to live,
you need to learn how to die.
Separate from your body while you are alive,
so you can more easily transition later.

Cubist Death of Socrates

Do not fear death,
for it is only another transformation.
You are not alone,
nor will you ever be alone,
because we are all one.
Add in the L from love and
alone becomes all one.
We will be with you
through every transformation,
at every turn.

A Sense of Being Stared At

Peel away the layers of yourself
and you'll go another level.
Deeper and deeper
until the watcher is far away
and you find yourself
at the center of the universe,
also at the edge.

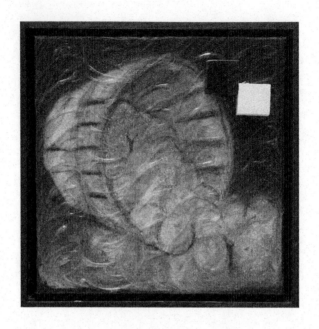

I Know What You're Thinking

Get to the core to find the truth.

Get down to the canvas

to where you first began.

Here you are full circle,

looking for meaning

before creation,

looking for meaning

after creation.

Seeker, the answers are inside.

These Truths are Self-Evident

Sink into the uncomfortable place
and feel its experience.
There are beings in other worlds
that wish they had emotion
and can only feel it through you.
So feel it full-throttle.
It's in your nature!

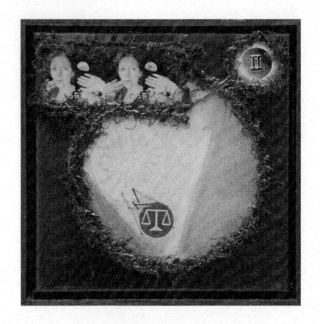

Gemini Moon

Stretch with your soul
to the far-reaches of the universe.
Reach past the furthest point in your imagination,
and then go further still.

There you will find the edge of reason and belief.

Spiral Dynamics with Shadow Self

This shadow needs tending
or the havoc will be strong enough
to push you into a dark delirium
of serious consequence.

Meet this dark collective and personal being.
Hold him close. Learn from his wisdom.

Summoning My Better Angels

She won't harden because
when you're done with the show,
she's out of here and back to the place
from where she was summoned.
Angels are temporary visitors,
not permanent muses or protectors.

Here, There Be Dragons

Seek because it brings you places
and keeps you curious.
But know that not all things are knowable
and there are questions you will still have in the end.

Find the unanswerable questions
and take a guess.

Spirit loves when you guess!

Transformation in Progress

Know that feeling when you look in the mirror

and don't fully recognize yourself?

That's your spirit saying, hey,

I'm just hanging out in this body for a while.

I know it's strange but don't sweat it.

The journey doesn't last too long

and you're guaranteed

to learn a few things.

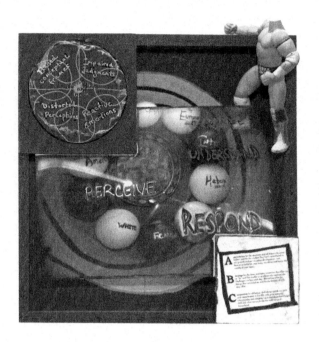

My Oppression Ain't Pretty

Your unique voice is what's required

to elevate humanity

to its next level

of conscious evolution.

Be empowered by that voice.

Let it rise up to help others

gather their strength.

There is work to do.

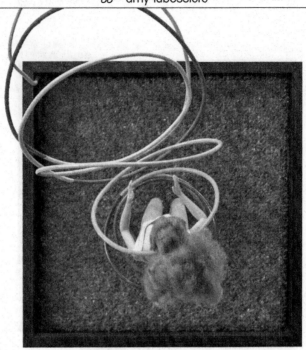

Hooping the Spiralectic

Journey along the spiral

of your own life's making.

Go back and forth

and see where you've been.

Journey on the vortex

of the path that is before you.

Do not forget where you're coming from.

You'll need to remember it

when you get to where you're going.

Chapter Seven:
Expect the Unexpected

"The greatest act of courage is to be and to own all
of who you are — without apology, without excuses,
without masks to cover the truth of who you are."

- Debbie Ford

Expect the Unexpected

In the years following my participation in the Conscious Evolution program, I enjoyed living as a sober woman. For the first year or so, we attended 12-step meetings regularly. I volunteered to help Tao manage the ArtSpace Gallery and assist with the art business. Tao and I were also spending more time at Still Waters, his childhood home. We got engaged on the night of the new moon, Valentine's Day and Chinese New Year.

Many years ago, after Tao and his sisters Zen and Chi left the property for school and life ventures, Tao's mother Mavis and father Paul got divorced. Mavis lived at the property and rented out a cottage or two for years afterward. But the buildings began to decline and upkeep took much time and money. His parents were considering the sale of the property.

I looked around and said to Tao, "hey, maybe we should turn this into a retreat center."

Tao's eyes lit up. We started dreaming out loud. We envisioned what retreats could look like. We imagined helping others to move their enlightened pursuits further in the world. We imagined a place where like-minded people could come together to heal themselves and help the world. In that moment, the energy was put in motion. Little did I know how much work there would be or what would happen.

By the time Tao and I took over the property, the cottages, guest house and recreation hall were full of junk and uninhabitable. The main house was full of clutter and the oldest part of the house was significantly deteriorated. The main house is situated as the focal point of the property.

All the energy flows through this building and radiates out to the 88 acres of conservation land and the 12-acre pond.

A few steps from the main house is the studio, also known as the recreation hall. The healing vibe from that corner is palpable. On the other side of the main house is the Guest House with five guest bedrooms upstairs and the future large event space downstairs.

We cleaned out The Party Room, Cottage One, The Rec Hall (that we now called The Art & Yoga Studio) and opened as a sober retreat center.

Working part time over two years, we hosted many different types of groups that came to create their own retreats, such as: Wounded Warriors, Men's 11th Step Recovery, Christian Women's Mission, Art-Making for Women, and Kundalini Yoga. Once we hosted a Buddhist group in full robes. We hosted wild mushroom foraging presentations, autumnal yoga classes, aromatherapy chakra balancing sessions, and more. Once a woman brought 22 friends and hosted a wedding-dress-burning fire ritual retreat.

After a while, I stopped going to 12-step meetings. I had it all figured out and thought I had grown enough. My spiritual enrichment had slowed and life was busy. I was happy where I was.

Tao and I had a two-person art show at Hartford ArtSpace Gallery. It was also a Jack-and-Jill celebration for our future wedding. We were dressed to the nines with a black-and-red color theme. Our artwork filled the gallery. About an hour into the party, I snuck upstairs with three girlfriends to show them my wedding dress. I put it on.

"Let's go," I told Carol Ann, Valerie and Christine.

"Beautiful dress, Amy! Where are we going with you dressed like that," Carol Ann said, "You're going to show everyone your wedding dress?"

"No," I said. "We are getting married. This is a surprise wedding." My friends were thrilled. We had a blast. Our DJ, Ken and Tao's sister Zen were in on our plot. Everyone else was shocked. My mother-in-law Mavis thought it was performance art. We were married in a beautiful and sober celebration. Life continued on.

One night, I drove to Fairfield, CT to hear a talk by David Wolfe, a well-known nutritionist and raw foods guru. A neighbor at ArtSpace told me about David years ago. I read a few of his books, and he was a featured presenter in my health coaching training. David is an inspiring source of information and inspiration. He talks about cutting-edge health practices and living the best life ever. I approached him after his talk and he recalled meeting me the year before. I invited him and his crew to come to Still Waters sometime in the future.

The day after I attended David's talk, I was tired from the long drive and lecture. Tao and I had tickets to TheaterWorks in Hartford to opening night of *I Loved, I Lost, I Ate Spaghetti*, by local playwright Jacques Lamarre. I was distracted and stuck in my thoughts. I walked through the studio, smashed my foot on the bottom of a metal ladder and heard a crunching sound. Fuck. That. Really. Fucking. Hurt. I managed to ice it and get dressed for the play. I sat in the theater, my right ankle resting on my left thigh, pinky toe throbbing. If you've ever broken a toe, you know how painful it can be. I was laughing hard at Jacques' hilarious play while in excruciating pain. Perhaps it was a sign of the juxtaposition of what was to come.

The next day, Tao and I went to the Saturday walk-in clinic at my doctor's office. They sent me for an x-ray and we drove over Avon Mountain. The radiologist conferred with me, even though it wasn't official and she wasn't allowed, that there was a crack on my fifth metatarsal. Ouch. My toe was broken. I decided to exclaim to everyone that I broke my foot because this hurt so bad it was deserving of the bigger declaration.

As Tao drove, I looked at him and pointed to a liquor store. I said, "Hey, you want to get a bottle of wine and watch a movie?

"Yeah," he said. "Let's do that."

Tao pulled into the parking lot and I asked him to go in and get some Chardonnay. He did. We drank that night. I spent the next two years drinking my face off. Just like that, my sobriety was gone.

Stuffing my feelings and masking pain with alcohol after years of sobriety is what recovering alcoholics call a relapse. I stayed there for nearly two years.

Part of me thought that alcoholism as a disease was bullshit. Drinking was a matter of willpower and control, and those that couldn't do either were simply not willing to. I was drinking again and was happy with my life. I guess it wasn't that bad before. I was managing things just fine. Work was going along and new opportunities were coming our way. Everything was fine except when it wasn't.

In November of that year, Tao and I decided that I would shift my marketing and management efforts to his art business and we would continue to host small retreats at Still Waters. My part-time work at the marketing firm was changing. They needed someone full-time, and another colleague was ready to step in from her part-time position. I was ready to move on. We decided that my contract would end in the first week of December.

The following week, Tao was at a routine annual doctor's appointment and got some unsettling news. "There is a strong murmur in your heart," his doctor said. "You need to see a cardiologist." We scheduled his appointment a few weeks out.

Despite all of the regular evening wine drinking, I did manage to squeeze in some self-improvement attempts along the way. I could be in denial of the deep-seated problem — my drinking — and focus on other issues.

Tao and I participated in The Landmark Forum, a weekend intensive educational experience designed to crack open our issues and propel our lives forward. We already had it scheduled and paid for, so we participated. The Forum helped me immensely, especially to clear out misconstrued perceptions I had about my father and help me to establish a wonderful adult relationship with him that continues to this day.

Part of the Landmark deal is that when you complete the Forum, you can participate in a future 10-week seminar. So I jumped right into a seminar on Creating Miracles.

Over the next few weeks, Tao was napping a lot and sometimes sleeping 16 hours a day. We were going to various appointments and he was getting test after test to see what the problem was. Tao is the kind of man that often works 16 hours a day and to see him sleep like that triggered me that he was going to die. All my unprocessed pain from the loss of Charlie rose to the surface.

Our lives quickly unraveled. Turns out, Tao's heart and blood vessels were clear but he desperately needed an aortic valve replacement. His body was declining quickly. We wondered how we didn't see this coming. He had been tired a lot lately but we didn't expect anything like this.

We had insurance but it was the cheap and basic kind — it was what we could afford on an artist's inconsistent income. This was a time before insurance was a requirement and there was no Obamacare. We had a $12,000 deductible and 30% coinsurance ahead of us. I didn't know how we would pay for this. I could drink my wine to escape but my solid income from the consultancy job was gone. We needed a miracle.

In the Creating Miracles seminar, we pondered a question in the group: What would be something unreasonable for you to create? I thought long and hard but the mission was clear: Raise $20,000 for Tao's Open Heart Surgery. This was a tall order. Tao and I created fundraisers before. Un+Art was a successful fundraising art show we produced together four times, and at its most successful we raised $2,200 for South Park Inn Homeless Shelter.

Several months later, a week before Tao's scheduled surgery, *Art for the Open Heart* had its opening reception. Hundreds of artists agreed to participate and we hung the work in Hartford ArtSpace Gallery. Even though we had a blizzard and state of emergency that evening, 50 people showed up for the reception. Roads were shut down and people came anyway; several people snow-shoed in from West Hartford. People donated and purchased artwork. I quickly shifted the one-night-only reception into a series of weekend events. The next night, hundreds of people came out. A Gallery record-breaking fifty works of art were sold. Many artists donated all of the funds from the sale, even though we encouraged them all to keep a percentage for themselves. Along with a crowd-funding campaign, I exceeded my goal. The universe provided what we needed to pay our bills.

The surgery was a flawless success. Tao's heart was healed. We began the road to financial recovery and life continued on. A few weeks later, Tao got back to work slowly and surely. We started to rebuild our lives. The art business continued. Still Waters continued. We seemed to be back on an upward swing, wine and all.

Chapter Eight: Through the Fire

♥

"I'm burning up, burning up for your love."

- Madonna

Through the Fire

The morning was calm and tranquil at Still Waters. Breakfast was simple — bowls of organic oatmeal with Vermont maple syrup and a pinch of pink salt. Hot coffee with cream and stevia in a hand-thrown mug created by a local artist. Crisp spring air. A light mist rose from the pond. The birds were singing. Mourning doves sang. Finches flew in the cool breeze.

The entire spring day and retreat center season was before us, ready to unfold with all of its spectacular opportunity. I could feel it in the air. I let the dogs run outside. Maggie, our black lab, ran up the hill into the woods, then circled back down to the pond to go for a swim. BeeBe, our white rescue miniature poodle, romped close by, always in view of me. I could feel the spring air on my face. Just a slight chill. The sun was peeking out of puffy clouds and streaming onto the pond.

As I sipped my coffee, I thought about the day's schedule. It was Sunday, but that was never our day of rest because we had no staff. It was just us. There was always more to do. Our agenda for the day was grounds keeping work for Tao and his assistant Keith, and marketing outreach for me.

The night before, I posted a cool video of the pond's waterfall on Facebook. I was drinking copious amounts of Chardonnay and thinking about the retreat season ahead. My illness was progressing. I had no interest in stopping drinking. I thought my life was manageable up to this point. Moderate wine drinking without consequences was all that I wanted.

Tao and I were in a celebratory work mode. We had some advanced reservations of various small groups. It was our third year of hosting retreats at Still Waters and we were doubling our part-time small business each year. We had not become profitable, but I was optimistic that we might get to a point where income could at least match our expenses for the ongoing improvements to this sacred place.

Anticipation was building for the upcoming season and all the work needed to prepare the buildings and grounds. We were bootstrapping. Every dollar we earned in our mural and art business, as well as my marketing consulting business, was allocated to our modest living expenses or as capital contributions for Still Waters improvements. We had already invested nearly $60,000 into rebuilding Cottage Duality, and much more around the property. Managing and funding Still Waters was part of our lives now. We were committed to it.

Tao, Keith and I were in the main house this particular morning. I was clearing the table of breakfast bowls and they were getting ready to do some outdoor tasks. Tao was thrilled when we had the budget to hire a helper. "Many hands make light work," we'd repeat like a mantra.

As I brought our breakfast bowls over to the sink, I smelled something burning. The wood stove isn't on, I thought to myself.

"Hey guys," I said, "What is that smell?"

Tao was used to comments like that from me and knew it could have been anything. Nothing unusual was happening. I walked into the living room. That part of the house had wide, uneven wood floor planks. The floor sloped in unpredictable directions. Dirt collected in the irregular cracks. At that moment when the smell was intensifying, the faintest smoke was rising through the floorboards like a thin whisper of a ghost. I wondered why there was smoke rising from the floor. There was no room in my brain to understand that a fire could be happening inside the house.

"Hey guys," I said, "why is there smoke rising from the floor?"

"What?!" Tao yelled, then he ran into the living room.

"Holy Shit," he shouted, and he ran toward the basement.

"Keith, get all of the fire extinguishers!" he shouted. Then he looked at me and said calmly and directly, "Amy, call the fire department!"

I grabbed my phone and opened the Google app. I typed in "Voluntown Fire Department." My brain was not thinking it was an emergency. A fire could not be happening. This was something else. "Voluntown Fire Department," the man answering the phone stated flatly.

"I think my house is burning, my house is on fire," I spoke quickly and nervously, unsure of the present moment.

"What is your address, " he asked. I gave it.

Then he said quickly, "Everyone out of the house, and call 911!"

I called 911 as the surreal experience was escalating. The smoke swiftly and thickly filled the building like a dense fog on a massive lake. I searched for my miniature poodle BeeBe and found her quickly, as she was almost always following me around. I scooped her up and held her on my hip like a baby while I hurried upstairs (quite foolishly). I was a bit hung over and dehydrated from last night's wine binge. I was not thinking clearly. I figured I had time to grab some stuff. I had not experienced a house fire from the inside. The quick pace with which smoke fills a building is astounding. Out of the corner of my eye, I spotted our hand-sculpted wedding cake topper — adorned with Tao's face and mine, a butterfly and a dragon. Our incredibly talented artist friend, Julia Ambrose, sculpted it. As I grabbed it, I noticed it was broken (an ominous sign).

I ran around upstairs and found my laptop, small makeup bag and a pair of jeans. I was still in pajamas — yoga pants and a tee shirt.

The smoke was rising. It was chasing me around the house, coiling around corners, expanding and growing, as if it were teasing the house and me with its presence. But this was no game. The clock was ticking, and a deadly force was nipping at my heels. My heart was pounding and my head started to ache. The smell was getting worse. As I approached the stairs, about to descend with my hands full, I saw the smoke ascending the risers like a menacing wave. Hands full, I hurried down out of the smoke-filled building.

One never knows how we will deal with extremely stressful situations and what will be important to us. None of the stuff really mattered, just the people and dogs. By the way, where the hell was Maggie? Our rescue black lab, sweet submissive Maggie was always bumbling around, gleefully running for the pond or schlumping like Eeyore. My memories of the fire do not include her. I have no idea where she was.

At that point, Tao was in the basement confronting the fire. From the living room, he opened the basement door, fire extinguishers in his arms. The stairwell was smoke-filled and white. Tao cautiously stepped down the rough, plywood stairs and felt the heat rising. As his feet hit the basement floor, he saw the searing, hot flames. It was like an upside-down river of flaming hot hell on the ceiling. He set the four extinguishers down on the dirt floor and sprayed each one at the fire trying to find the source. He almost thought he had it beat. He had exhausted every fire extinguisher in the house. But the fire continued its wrath.

I was outside and rushed to the propped-open bulkhead door and screamed into the billowing smoke, "We've got to get out of here," I screamed.

The moment was terrifying. Tao wanted to save this house, his childhood home, his family homestead, and the place we were trying like hell to bootstrap into our retreat center business. Built in 1730, the old side of the building was going up in flames like a wooden match. At this point, smoke filled the entire house, including the newer side constructed in the 1940s and the other section built by Tao's Dad in the '80s. The house was a hybrid of various structures all clunked together into its own weird and wonderful personality.

On this quiet Sunday morning, the smoke was traveling like a poisonous snake, slow and low, yet fast and twisting, getting into every nook and corner, filling every bit of existence until it started seeping into the walls and out the cracks between the windows and the building. From the outside, it looked like a thick, soupy fog was migrating out of the house and into the yard.

Once outside, I headed to my car, a 2006 VW Rabbit. BeeBe and I got in. Time was moving in slow motion. Like the moment of a car accident when everything slows down as the car crushes into itself and everything changes.

I moved the car next to the sauna and pond to leave the driveway clear for the fire truck. I looked around and saw Keith. He sat down at a nearby picnic table and stared off into the distance. I wondered if Tao was okay. I was afraid of him getting hurt or killed in the fire. I could not believe that this was all happening.

Tao emerged from the house. I exhaled. Smoke steamed off his clothing, as if he was also burning. He walked down the hill from the house. Tao was looking toward the street for the firefighters, anxiously awaiting their arrival.

"Where the fuck are they?" he muttered hopelessly.

During a traumatic moment, time moves sluggishly. Seconds feel like minutes and minutes feel like hours. From across the driveway, I looked at Tao's eyes to see if I could sense what he was feeling. I saw devastation and resignation. I am not sure if he had those emotions in that moment, but I certainly did. This moment was not in my plans.

I heard sirens.

About thirty fully geared up firefighters ran in, dragging hoses, carrying axes and equipment. They fought and the fire blazed on. More people arrived. Some went inside, others hovered close by. Others walked back and forth to their trucks at the end of the long driveway. It took much effort get the fire contained.

As I sat in my car, I looked at their faces and felt a security in knowing this is something they do all the time. My feeling of devastation and defeat as they rushed into my home was like nothing I had ever experienced before nor want to experience again. I had no idea the long and extensive journey before me.

Five towns responded that day. We were quite blessed that the Voluntown Fire Department was practicing drills that morning and responded quickly. The department is mostly volunteer men and women, so if it wasn't a Sunday at 9:15 am, and was during the week, most of the firefighters would have been out of town at work. I later heard that someone thought my emergency call was a prank because people usually call 911 when there is a fire, not the firehouse directly.

While the firefighters did their thing, I searched my glove compartment looking for the insurance company's phone number. I realized it wouldn't be in my car. I grabbed my phone and searched through my emails to find the number for my insurance agent. I didn't have a notebook handy so I grabbed a postcard I had for the Copper Beech Institute (CBI) introducing their new mindfulness-based retreat center in West Hartford, CT. I thought this was a good sign that everything would be okay. I met executive director Brandon Nappi a few months prior and admired the programs he was creating for the community.

My insurance agent Dave picked up when I called his cell. I jotted down phone numbers and notes. The list making began. We had to get an emergency services provider to come and secure the house. We needed a public adjuster to help us work with the insurance company. Dave told me I should update family and let them know what happened and that we were okay. This moment felt similar to when a family member dies and tasks show up while you're in the middle of grief. While it's not the same trauma, the surreal energy makes everything feel like a dream. My hangover and dehydrated body compounded the issue. The feeling was crap.

At one point, Jody, the Voluntown Fire Chief, told us we were very lucky the fire happened in the morning when it did. If it happened a few hours earlier, we might not have detected it while sleeping, and it likely would have killed us.

Fire creeps around silently. It didn't dissipate until every crevice of the house was filled and then emptied again. It didn't stop until every smoldering ash was extinguished. It took five towns of firefighters five hours to put out the fire. Finally, as the birds sang sweetly and the clouds gently covered the afternoon sun over our land, it was over.

After the firefighters left, Keith took our truck home to West Hartford. Tao and I stood there, alone. We looked at each other and shook our heads. My thoughts were reeling. This was a shitty situation. Of course, it could have been worse. It can always be worse. No one died, thank God. This was just material stuff. Everything is replaceable, except time. Our business would get delayed. Things would get complicated. Life was giving us our turn at a pile of uncomfortable lessons and me a significant bout of spiritual misgivings. It was time to move forward. I wanted this situation quickly resolved.

In the weeks that followed the fire, I was an emotional tornado. My daily wine drinking reflected that as my inner feelings of hopelessness and despair intensified; I was losing what little control I had. The fire had ruined me. I had to cancel four retreats reserved for the summer. Writing those refund checks was hard because now I was failing on paper. I thought that maybe we could fix the problem and get things resolved in a couple of months. I had no idea what the universe had in store.

There were a few nights that Tao suggested we ease up on the wine drinking. When two people are downing a magnum and a half of Chardonnay, sometimes two full magnums on a Wednesday night, there is trouble. Every few days, we would get into some irrational screaming matches, more power struggles, fueled by excessive wine. I suppose that therapist we had years ago was right.

We were both emotionally exhausted. When Tao suggested we slow down, I agreed. But I was lying. I would drink that night, and the next, and the next. Every sip wasn't enough. The rest of the bottle wasn't enough. This was the alcoholic progression discussed in 12-step meetings.

"How do you know an alcoholic is lying? Her lips are moving."

This popular joke in recovery is surprisingly true on many levels. Recovery requires honesty, willingness and desperation.

I was delusional and denied my delusions. As time went on, the pain was increasing exponentially. My alcoholism was moving forward. It was escalating the whole time, even while I was sober. Here I was, almost to that line of no choice.

In recovery circles, I heard stories from people who talk about morning drinking. This was one of my fears. I'm not talking about the "hair of the dog" morning drinking type of imbibing, the Sunday late morning Bloody Mary with the organic celery and olives in a tall glass. I am talking about the dark and dirty kind of morning drink, the dregs of the bottles scattered on the floor at the end of a party, the bottoms of other peoples glasses that still had liquor in them. Grabbing at them desperately, seeking fulfillment and something to take away the dark, unnamed pain at the core of my soul. That 6:00 am bottle of vodka that seems like a good idea. That uncontrollable shaking, unable to hold the glass steady, waiting to sip the liquor the mind and body craves like a vampire, ready to kill for the next sip of blood; a sticky feeling of my filthy, swollen face after a night of sweating; the precious body desperately trying to rid itself of alcohol poisoning. That was real fear. I was standing on the edge of that becoming my life.

I came close to that fear one morning. I woke up with a terrible hangover after a night of binge drinking Chardonnay. This would often entail drinking one or two regular bottles or up to a magnum of wine. I never knew how much I would consume on any given night. How much was in the house?

I walked into the bathroom and looked in the mirror. I did not recognize my own face. It was entirely swollen. My eyes were slits and my lids were like puffballs. My cheeks were a grayish color and my face was fat and bloated. I looked a decade older and like total shit. I thought I was having an allergic reaction to something I ate. Did I drink too much? I don't recall. Maybe I had a little too much last night. I could handle this; I would muddle through.

A month after the fire, I was feeling even more desperate. I could no longer drink. I could no longer not drink — I was stuck in the middle of an emotional and physical nightmare. I had lost it all. One of the biggest problems an alcoholic has is lack of power. We want power and control so badly that we will do anything to try to bend the will of the universe toward us.

I thought maybe I needed to change everything (except me). I should quit this shit right away. "This shit" being my life. I was certain the problem was my family, my husband, my neighbors, my businesses and my shitty-ass life. Wallowing in a swamp of self-pity, I had could not see or feel the blessings, love and grace that surrounded me. The alcohol was sinking me into a dark, miserable pit of horrific despair.

One of my Facebook friends posted "6 years" as her status update. Because I had been in a 12-step recovery program before, I knew what she meant. She was six years sober. I had a tiny little window of clarity in that moment. Wow. Maybe I needed to get back in recovery.

Some of the recovery ideas and slogans came rushing back to me.

Easy Does It.
One Day at a Time.
Live and Let Live.
Just for Today.

Shit. I don't know if I want to do this again. It's too fucking hard. There goes all my fun. Wait a minute. Was I having fun? No, I was miserable.

I called my friend Christine.

"Hey Chris," I said, "I have a real problem and I think I have to come back to the rooms."

She said, "Oh Amy, I am so happy to hear that. You know what? I am speaking tonight and I haven't done so in 12 years. Will you come? It's a women's meeting in Rocky Hill."

I really couldn't say no at that point. I asked for help, she answered, and I wasn't going to worm my way out of it. I could feel the deep internal struggle. Part of me wanted to say fuck it, just keep going. You can still function. You aren't living under a bridge and you aren't in jail. You can still drink. It's only wine. Didn't Jesus drink wine? I bet the Dalai Lama drinks wine.

I went to the meeting. I heard Christine share her experience, strength and hope. The circle of twenty-two women in recovery welcomed me back. I sat there, defeated and relieved. I started my journey, again — but in many ways for the first time.

It felt like I was on the precipice of losing everything. My marriage was spiraling out of control and I was ready to leave my husband, my businesses, and my family. My plan was to grab my dog, my laptop and a bag of clothes, empty my bank account and drive, probably to California. It seemed like a good idea to run away to the other side of the country. Who knows what would have happened if I had done that. The charms and privileges that have found me along my path would not have continued. My new life would have been working in a diner somewhere, unhappy and confused, drunk and scared, wondering what I had done. Instead, I got myself into recovery and learned how to feed the spiritual hunger.

The divine unfolding that comes from living a sober life and working on spiritual principles has been astonishing so far. There are still shit-storms and bad things because life happens, but they are easier to deal with because of what I learn and experience in sobriety. I have a set of spiritual tools I can access anytime. The experience certainly hasn't been perfect. But it has been an experience that's truly beyond my wildest dreams.

At the moment as I write this, I am 3.51 years sober. That's 42.16 months. 1,286 days. 30,848 hours and counting. One day at a time.

Part Two:
Lessons on the Path

Chapter Nine:
Beginner's Mind

♥

"We must be willing to get rid of the life we planned,
so as to have the life that is waiting for us. The old
skin has to be shed before the new one can come."

- Joseph Campbell

Beginner's Mind

Beyond emotional and spiritual devastation, the physical consequences of my drinking never caught up with me. My outsides looked just fine. My insides were a mess. And it didn't last forever. After a couple of years in sobriety, including a sober wedding, I relapsed. Luckily for me, I had the opportunity to reset my world in the experience of beginner's mind.

Beginner's mind is talked about in Zen Buddhist circles. While I don't know about the origins of it, the idea is common so everyone knows what it is. It is that time you see or notice something for the first time. We can consciously bring ourselves back to that state by shifting our awareness. I can softly ask myself to notice something as if I never saw it before. This is not a 100% accurate experience, but it is possible to trick the mind a bit and try to experience it authentically.

One day I was at home, snuggling with my miniature poodle, BeeBe. She is a rescue dog approximately 12 years old. She adores me and acts like my protector, following me around and making sure she keeps people around me in check. I look at her and try to imagine seeing her again but for the first time. She does not respond the way she did when I first met her. She's not in this game. But I can still notice her and subtlety shift my thinking that this is the first time I am ever seeing or petting her. What I realize is that this brings me into the present moment. Fully. Completely. I am here. What a relief it is not to be thinking about the past or projecting into the future, but rather being here right now, fully alive and aware in this moment.

Alcoholism is an illness that centers in my mind. It affects me spiritually, mentally, and physically. I have found that I can treat this issue with spiritual, mental and physical approaches. One of those approaches is beginner's mind. I return to beginner's mind when I see someone falling over drunk at a party. I consider those shoes. I was unaware I was wearing them for most of my adult life. I remember it when I see a newcomer at a 12-step meeting or when someone asks me for help.

Energy cannot be created or destroyed. But it can be redirected. Addiction and compulsion cannot be satisfied by something else unless it is of a similar nature. Anyone who experienced urges to drink, cravings for cigarettes or addictive drugs or the compulsion to eat refined sugar will understand.

For the alcoholic, wine, beer or booze takes the edge off like nothing else. This is why so many of us die tragic deaths while actively using our substance of choice. It is not a matter of having a strong willpower or moral fiber to just say no. Our substance has a stronger grip on us than these emotional and moral elements. Something else has to come into play. We have to be willing to slowly work on softening that sharp, metallic edge of un-fulfillment. Creativity is an alternative, especially when funneled through spirituality.

It helps to have self-knowledge and awareness of our situation, but that is also not enough. It is not like being addicted to strawberries. If I find out I am allergic to strawberries, I simply never eat them again. The consequences are clear and the choice is easy. Not so much for the alcoholic. If it was that easy no alcoholic or addict would ever have to die.

How many people have we known with alcoholism and/or addiction that are fully aware of their problem but use and die anyway? We are not necessarily suicidal. In Alcoholics Anonymous, the textbook for the 12-step recovery program, there is a chapter entitled More About Alcoholism. It states, "Alcoholics of our type are in the grip of a progressive illness. Over any considerable period we get worse, never better." (Page 30, *Alcoholics Anonymous*). When I read this for the first time, I didn't believe it. I had to hear other people share about their experience to hear the proof. Healing happens better when we are together. I cannot do this alone.

The point is not to destroy the feelings. The point is to be able to experience them. This, for me, required a spiritual experience to help me change. Can I simply be with what is? Can I accept the present moment without needing to change it or fix it? This is what stillness means, like a flower, perfectly still and alive. Still growing.

Returning to beginner's mind and early experiences reminds me what it was like when I was first trying to get sober. It was hard. I was trying to change from one habit, daily wine drinking, to another habit of not daily wine drinking. This was not easy, but as time goes on, I forget. Part of me wants to forget the uncomfortable experiences and live with ease in my new normal. In order to stay sober, I have to remember what it was like, or I will try to convince myself that a glass of wine is a good idea. If that happens all bets are off.

I do not want to see where active alcoholism will take me. I have no interest in matching stories with my friends and colleagues at 12-step meetings. I humbly acknowledge that if I don't stay sober, my life will eventually be a shit-storm. At minimum, my life would be an emotional pit of personal hell, and at maximum, a devastation of everything and everyone that I care about.

With this in mind, I trudge along with my tools of wise living: Healthy food, regular exercise, good sleep, a spiritual practice in 12-step living and good creative outlets.

It took me a couple of years to find what works for me, and it only works in this moment. My needs will change as life experience teaches me what I need to know for personal growth. For now, this works.

I am relatively happy, sober and alive. I have the ability to tackle huge projects with my partner, such as reviving Still Waters into an active retreat center. I can be supportive to my family and friends. I can manage the care of my elderly father-in-law. I can be a person in service to the rest of the world. There is no other job that makes sense to me right now.

My recovery is a looping sphere. It circles back around on itself, in a wave. My spirituality and recovery walk hand-in-hand. I don't always understand how or why, but my sobriety leads me closer to a God-like experience. The universe. The love that is everything in all creation. That which created you and me. That which can only be called God in its different names.

Chapter Ten:
Food Changes Everything

♥

"The body speaks its message louder and louder
trying to get what it needs, even as it does its best to
function with those needs unfulfilled."
- Charles Eisenstein, *The Yoga of Eating*

Food Changes Everything

We all have an inner compass that will guide us if we clear out the cobwebs. We can do this with diet and lifestyle. Eat more plants. Eliminate alcohol and other mind-altering substances, if they are problematic. Move our bodies to get stronger. Find our own creative path. Each of these choices, day by day, adds up to the cumulative effect of profound change.

How do we nourish ourselves? What does food have to do with anything? Does it matter? I have found that being conscious of what I consume — and how I consume it — is directly related to my quality of life. As they say: garbage in, garbage out.

This isn't how it was growing up. In childhood, my food intake was not a conscious event. I was blissfully unaware. I found much comfort in food, especially sweets. Mom would make delicious meals. Her Swedish pancakes were beyond comparison.

Mom had a talent for making gorgeous cakes. She would bake and decorate beautiful birthday cakes and painstakingly decorate them with patterns of tiny rosettes. For my 14th birthday, she made me a vanilla and chocolate giant roller-skate cake with the words "Keep on Rolling, Amy."

My family went out to eat once or twice a week close to home at the Town Line Diner. Mom and Charlie were friendly with the waiter, Alex, who wore a tuxedo every night. Alex was exquisitely mannered and quite charming. He'd always greet us with a polite, "hello and welcome!"

I usually ordered the most expensive thing on the menu. I was certain I would have the best if it cost the most. I am not sure where this mentality came from, but as a young adult, eating surf and turf with a baked potato and creamed spinach was not exactly the best dinner, though I could've done worse. Back then, food quality was better. There were not as many chemicals in our food.

Sometimes we would go to Dairy Barn, the drive-thru store that sold cigarettes, beer, ice cream and Entenmann's cakes. We would go in Mom's Cadillac or Charlie's Z28, and buy a box of frozen fried chicken. The box looked like a fat, oversized milk carton. The chicken always came out of the oven super-crispy.

During the years before Charlie's passing, Mom grew beautiful string beans, strawberries, tomatoes and cucumbers in the backyard garden. We ate some other vegetables, too. The asparagus was boiled until soft. We ate iceberg lettuce-based salads. That's just what you did in the '70s and '80s. Mom did the best she could for Nancy and me and I know it was pretty good for the time.

I also remember, I think it was after Charlie died, going to Arby's down the street and gorging myself on a beef and cheddar sandwich, hash browns and a chocolate shake. I was addicted to crappy food. I wasn't allowed to have soda as Mom said it would rot our teeth.

I didn't have a concept of what healthy was. Mom told us, "finish what is on your plate, there are starving kids in China." I wished I could give them some of my food. Eating everything meant I was doing well.

On a daily basis, I felt awkward and uncomfortable in my own skin. My clothing was on the dumpy side. Sometimes I went to school without a shower. I felt gross and chubby. I'm sure that left a bad impression on the other kids and impacted my non-existent popularity.

In sixth grade, a kid named Jerry made fun of me. Jerry played the trombone and was a smart, cute, and tall blonde boy. He was part of a group of kids that hung out at Wayne's house. Wayne was older and let the neighborhood kids hang out at his place. He had a pool table and was a neighbor to Jerry, who was in the junior high band and I thought was my friend.

One day, we were at Wayne's and Jerry was being a typical wisecracking jerk. He started picking on me. He told me my lips were pale and that no boy was going to be attracted to me. He told me my stomach was bigger than my chest and he laughed. I can still hear his evil, cackling laugh in my mind's ear. What I heard was: You are ugly and unlovable. No one will ever love you.

Those unexpected criticisms from a boy I thought was cute hurt me in unexpected ways. I felt extra uncomfortable and fat. His ideas scalded me, never to leave. Not even 35 years later, at a time when I have burned many other pathways in my mind.

In my 20s, I became a junk-food vegetarian. I ate copious amounts of packaged vegetarian food, including dry cereals, pasta and boxed macaroni and cheese. As long as I was not consuming anything with a face, I felt I was doing the right thing.

I was a lacto-ovo vegetarian. I allowed myself to eat eggs and cheese because I loved them and rationalized it was more ethical than eating animals. I shopped at health food stores for veggie burgers, falafel and whatever else that I could find. At the time, vegetarianism was only at the beginning stages of becoming mainstream, so the selection was slim and costly.

Most of the faux-meat products tasted like cardboard. The texture was repulsive and unfulfilling, like eating a sour sponge. The veggie burgers were trying too hard to taste like meat. I remember walking past the meat section in a regular grocery store and feeling physically nauseous.

It was the '90s, when I first came to Connecticut and was working at the *Hartford Planet* magazine. My husband Jeremy had an iguana named Gia that ate better than we did – she ate huge salads every day. I would smoke pot, drink wine and eat a junk-food vegetarian diet, thinking I was saving the world, one meal at a time. I was trying. I believe we all live that way. We do the best we can in the moment, even if we are not conscious in any way. We are trudging along.

My favorite thing to do was to smoke pot, watch *Sex & the City* reruns on VHS, and eat Cap'n Crunch cereal straight from the box. Cereal was vegetarian. I thought my diet was compassionate and healthy. That cereal was vitamin-fortified, after all. And marijuana is a plant.

At this part of my dietary journey, I found *Stop the Insanity*, a book by Susan Powter. Susan had a fun writing style. I loved her idea of an extremely low-fat diet. I tried and stuck with it with extreme determination. I started hiking every weekend and dropped 20 pounds. I was still drinking and smoking cigarettes and pot. I was unaware the partying was effecting my body and mind. I was unconscious about this aspect of self. It's like I had blinders on, unable to see my toxic, self-medicating behavior. It would take another two decades before I could start honestly looking at myself. In the meantime, I was slowly shifting my food behaviors. As my diet evolved, my thinking shifted. As my creativity grew, my mind changed. I was peeling back of the layers of self. All of these elements contributed to my personal growth. This was holistic personal evolution.

Around the time of my super low fat, high-carbohydrate, high-sugar, cigarette and pot-smoking wine-drinking lifestyle, I began a serious venture into running. I got addicted to the high from a three-mile run. I started training for the Hartford half marathon. I was determined. I was likely the only one of thousands who ran a half marathon, then moments after crossing the finish line, lit up a Camel Light. I had addictions that needed filling. Sugar. Nicotine. Endorphins from running. Sex. Alcohol. Pot.

I lived this way for years. As my first marriage and life began to unravel, my creative self began to emerge again. I tried to claw my way out of my emotional misery with anything outside of myself. I had no idea that emotional and spiritual excavation was going to be the only way out. The only way out was in. The only way in was through.

Eventually, I stopped smoking pot because it was getting in the way of my drinking. I remember the last time I smoked.

It was one particular 4th of July. Tao and I were having a party at Still Waters. We weren't hosting retreats yet, but we had a bunch of friends over for camping and frivolity. I had been drinking wine all night. Ken was there. He came over to my tent around midnight and said, "Hey, want to smoke?" He lit up a joint and passed it to me. It felt good. I loved smoking and consciously knew it was toxic. I didn't care.

After smoking the joint, I went into a blackout. I woke up in my tent at sunrise. Tao was asleep next to me on the air mattress, our dog Maggie snoring. My head was pounding. It was a gorgeous morning. Yet I felt like an ax was stuck in my skull. I was still drunk. All I could think was: I have to stop smoking pot. And I quit, just like that. Alcohol wouldn't be so easy. King Alcohol had me as his devoted slave. He was pleased I released the pot from my daily practice. There was now more room for me to devote to him, my obsession.

Many years later, I was halfway through the master's degree program. I had found recovery (or did it find me?) and had stopped drinking. I saw a Facebook post by Corrina Richards, a well-known area yoga teacher and health coach. She was hosting an online food detox course. Hmmm. I *could* do that, I thought. I *should* do that. I could lose some weight, improve my skin and maybe feel a little better. I wasn't drinking so that part would be easy. Maybe it would help me stay sober. I signed up for the course.

In the course, I learned how to make my first green smoothie. I remember being apprehensive about it. It was as if my soul knew that the green drink would begin to transform my life and send me on a whole new path. We were encouraged to move and start some kind of physical practice. I started practicing Bikram Yoga.

As I continued on the three-week food detox plan, I knew I wanted to eventually become a health coach. I wanted what Corrina had. The day my official Master of Arts diploma arrived in the mail, I signed up for nutrition school at The Institute for Integrative Nutrition (IIN).

I jumped into the holistic health coach training at IIN in New York City. By the following year, I completed all the modules and was a certified holistic health coach, educated in more than 100 dietary theories. I was sober. I ate more plants. I was changing physically, mentally, emotionally, spiritually and creatively. All the elements of the psycho-spiritual life wheel were turning. I was filling up the God-sized hole I had inside with gratifying, non-toxic things.

The best way I could help others would be to learn how to take care of myself. I wanted to study all the dietary theories I could. That experience was amazing. The connections made at IIN with remarkable people from all over the world were life changing. The ability to become a health coach, open a retreat center and contribute in some small way to humanity is a tremendous gift.

Since then, I have taken other courses, seminars, and motivational programs and read many books. As a life-learner, I will continue to learn and grow on this journey to the best of my ability. I am so fortunate for this gift of life and must ensure that I live with love and gratitude, pointing toward the creative intelligence in the universe and sharing as much of it as possible.

Perhaps it is evident by now, but sometimes I take things to the extreme. My willpower is strong. I push to get it done. It is in my nature. I learned that an 80/20 rule is best. Eighty percent of the time, I eat the best food ever — organic, locally sourced, non-GMO, plant-based, grass-fed, as nature created it. Twenty percent of the time, I eat the other stuff. Now, I am not talking about going to a crappy fast food place and shoving in low-vibration burgers and fries. My Arby's days are long gone. McDonald's is just a place to pee and grab a black coffee while on a road trip. I'm talking about going to a local restaurant that makes great food and eating anything I want. It is about supporting another small business without it having to be on par with the latest optimal health specification and eating parameters. Enjoyment is about sometimes letting go. If I had a major health issue, I would take a different stance. But as a healthy, happy woman in her late 40s, an 80/20 philosophy serves me well.

Even though I am making positive health choices personally, the world is in crisis.

Consumers are becoming more aware of the impact food choices are making on their health and the greater good. Many documentaries and books exist to educate the public about these concerns. Consumers are being told how inhumane, corrupt and unjust our food system is, based on getting massive amounts of cheap, nutrient-deficient food to people. This is a profits-before-people system. It is broken.

My personal choices can help the world. I am making a statement with how I spend my money. I can think about purchasing high-quality, organic food and spend more of my income on food, rather than trying to buy the cheapest food possible. I can go to a farm and buy from the farmer or farmer's market. I can grow my own food anywhere.

I can embrace the sense of being part of something larger than myself — a movement of consciously evolving individuals. We are considerate. We are observing. We are thinking. We are mindful. We are compassionate. We care about the rest of the planet.

I answer the call to change — to change my choices of how I consume and how I think about the world. I cannot expect a shift overnight. I can go on a journey in a process of becoming, being and letting go. It is a continuous process that I must allow myself to carry out into the world and influence others. Each of us, when we are ready to hear the message, must answer this call. We must answer it for evolution and for humanity.

There are many excellent books and courses on the popular subject of food and healing. The most important thing is simply to begin the journey. This is how life gets better. I keep an open mind whenever possible. I listen to the universe whenever possible. I try to take Good Orderly Direction from the cosmos by listening with my heart. I keep willingness in my heart. I hold the desire to learn, to change and to be inspired by others. My mind has an openness to be wrong about everything that I thought was true.

Chapter Eleven:
Self-Care When I'm Too Busy

•

"Sometimes it's hard to tell where your
instincts start and your baggage stops."

- Rory Freedman

Self-Care When I'm Too Busy

Life is stuffed full of craziness. When I worked full-time, I surprisingly had more time to carve out all the things that had to be done. Or perhaps my life structure created an illusion. I had too much to do and no time to be sick. The most important thing I always needed is self-care. I don't mean jet-off-to-somewhere-when-you-can't-afford-it kind of self-care. I mean setting priorities on your own health and wellbeing. Period. No excuses. This sometimes requires crafty rearranging of schedules.

As a self-employed serial entrepreneur (that sounds fancy and highly profitable. Believe me, it is not), I juggle a million details at once. When I get overloaded, I know it's time to slow down. I take a pause and deep breath. I realign myself with my higher power and internal connection to the divine. I do not need any fancy courses or products to do this. Just a regular deep breath will do. Then I get on with things.

When this isn't enough, and it often isn't, I check my weekly schedule. Am I getting to 12-step meetings? Am I getting in at least three intense workouts or daily lighter activity each week? Am I having any lighthearted fun? All of these items need a resounding yes. Because as a former advertising employer used to say, if we're not having fun, we're doing it wrong. That's not to say that life is all fun and games. However, there needs to be the energy of hopefulness, playfulness, fulfillment and love underneath everything that I do.

The other day, I was at my desk working on the Art of Tao website. I looked at the time. "Oh shit, it's 11:05 a.m.," I said to myself. Boot camp starts in 25 minutes. I was not ready. I scrambled for my gym clothes, got dressed, filled my backpack and ran out the door. I made it. The class was grueling. Afterward, my body was spent — tired yet strong. It was worth the scramble. I didn't have time but I made the time.

The ongoing saga of my life includes care for my elderly father-in-law, Paul. A couple of weeks ago, we landed him a great apartment in a super independent and assisted living facility near our art studio in Hartford. Last night, while at Still Waters preparing the main house for reopening, I got a call from the facility that Paul fell. The nurse said he wasn't hurt, but that they had to let us know. Three hours later, another nurse called and said Paul couldn't walk. He had to go to the hospital because he can't stay there if he is unable to ambulate in the bathroom or get to the dining room.

An ambulance took Paul to the ER. Tao and I met him there. Right away, Paul lied about what happened.

"I don't remember," was all he said, with any question that made him uncomfortable. Since Paul has slight dementia, he probably didn't know all the answers, but he was covering up other aspects of the situation.

We returned to the art studio, and I woke up repeatedly throughout the night to check my phone in case the hospital called. All of this drama would likely push elements of needed support out the window. I might make excuses: no time for meetings, or workouts. But again, it is time to slow down: To feel the feelings, sip some coffee or tea, get to a meeting and go to the gym, or take a walk. There is no such thing as too busy. I must carve out the time. Life wants me to choose this for myself. I cannot show up for others if I don't show up for myself.

In my mind, I pour sumptuous bubble baths in my perfectly clean and clutter-free bathroom, with lavender-scented candles burning and soft music playing. There is a stack of fresh, clean towels and a beautiful purple robe waiting for me. Luxury and cleanliness surrounds my space. This is definitely not the art studio, but it is my self-care fantasy. I need more self-care, please.

Sometimes a change in perspective is needed. If you can get to a retreat, that is great. Stepping out of your life for a weekend or a couple of days mid-week is a great way to get aligned with self. Then you can go back to serving others in your life, in whatever that way shows up for you.

Kripalu and Omega Institute are wonderful centers that attract thousands of guests every year. They are costly but if you have the money and time, check them out. They host larger groups so their programming is expansive. You can also find smaller centers by searching online or asking friends for recommendations. There are websites like FindTheDivine.com that advertises and lists all sorts of retreat centers.

Or look for holistic local publications. In Connecticut, we have *Natural Awakenings* and *Natural Nutmeg*. By googling specific phrases of interest, you can find everything from silent meditation retreats in the mountains, to naked goddess snorkeling retreats in the Caribbean. Or just a simple bed and breakfast somewhere.

When you go, take a bunch of pictures when you get there and then shut off your cell phone if you can stand it. Please try. We are all so addicted to our technologies that we don't often realize it. You can check in the evenings if needed, but taking a few days off is ideal. Many bed and breakfast owners or retreat centers are happy to give you their phone number for any family member emergencies, if necessary. Unplug for God's sake and your own life reset.

Self-care can also show up as simple food choices. Add in an extra vegetable, or have the fruit instead of a cookie. Or have the cookie if that looks more like self-care. My mother calls me cookie. Her mother called her cookie. No one else calls me cookie, but I love cookies. If I allowed the world to know me better, everyone would call me cookie.

Sometimes we default into our old ways. All of a sudden, the 6:00 a.m. wake-up time turns into 7:15 am. We are not up for that workout, or green smoothie. We don't feel like choosing the next right thing. We want to call in sick or call it all off. It's okay. We don't have to spiral down into a rabbit hole of negative habits and behaviors. Allow the deviance, and as soon as possible, begin again.

There is a saying in sober circles and 12-step meetings, *progress not perfection*. When I shoot for perfection, I always fall short. When I shoot for progress, I always meet my mark. My weekly visits to the gym reflect this. Every time I struggle with real push-ups, with my elbow close to my side, I get a little bit stronger.

By the way, for years I was doing pushups wrong. I bent my arms like a chicken wing, bowing them out to the side. There was no way I was pushing up from my knees. I work out. I'm doing it with straight legs. Well, when I got honest with myself and realized I could be screwing up my shoulders with my fake pushups, I began to work on the real-deal ones. Now, I'm on my knees making slow progress every time. My pushups humble me.

We can get to the point where we are way too busy for anything. I understand this with the mountain of work in front of Tao and me to re-open Still Waters. Every little detail requires tending.

In those times of overwhelm, I pause. I realize there are only 24 hours in a day. I chunk my time into what needs doing, including self-care. Every little choice adds up over time: moments of meditation, healthy food choices, an exercise class, laughter with friends, making love with my husband, snuggling with my dog, a random act of kindness, saying yes, or saying no. All of our choices add up to create the tapestry of our beautiful and complex lives.

Chapter Twelve:
You Have a Responsibility

♥

"Art should comfort the disturbed and
disturb the comfortable."

- Banksy

You Have a Responsibility

"You have a responsibility with your skill," said Damon Honeycutt, one of the presenters that I met in the Conscious Evolution program. He was a swordsman, philosopher, painter, dancer with Pilobus and most notably, a martial artist. He was one of those people who definitively cultivated his skill. He found his passion and pursued it wholeheartedly.

Damon's words resonated with me. I have a responsibility with my skill. I am in awe of those that can find one thing: the painter that creates in one style, the writer that writes in one voice; or the actor that commits to her craft and works from being an extra for years until she gets leading roles and makes a living. The universe doesn't validate all of us. Not everyone does what he or she wants to do in the world. Sometimes we have to find what we want within whatever we are doing. We do the work from the inside out.

But what is my skill, anyway? My life keeps changing and my focus shifts. In any given chapter of my life, I might be good at one thing or another.

I love voiceover work. My first memory of noticing someone's voice was listening to the radio in my father's car. When I was a pre-teen, Dad picked us up on Sunday mornings, every other week and drove Nancy and me from our house in Huntington to his house in Islip.

Quite often, we listened to American Top 40, a radio show that played the top songs of the week, hosted by Casey Kasem. Casey's voice had style, uniqueness and a deep twang. Hosting a radio show was the coolest job ever, combining an actor's craft with a focus on the voice. I considered that as a future job, and kept it to myself.

Years later, when I moved to Connecticut, I found a volunteer gig at the East Hartford Public Library with *Talking Books*. They recorded books for the blind, print-disabled, and those who were unable to read.

I was moved and inspired. I thought about what it would feel like to be blind. I could not imagine it. I thought about Helen Keller and the amazing writing she accomplished in her life. She was a deaf and blind published author who earned a Bachelor of Arts degree. I thought how successful she was at life.

I thought about the people that I could help by volunteering. I thought about how lucky I was to be able to see.

I looked at the books in progress. There were always a few underway. The director told me that it took an entire year to record a regular novel. The volunteers would record it, and then more volunteers would review it for issues, re-record and review again, until the book was perfect.

My volunteer job was in the library's back room, where they had a small recording studio. I was a reviewer. I put on the massive headphones, grabbed a clipboard and picked up where the last reviewer left off. We followed stringent Library of Congress guidelines. I listened for incorrectly pronounced words, lip smacks and weird pacing. Sometimes it frustrated me that we had to be so perfect, but the director told me that they were funded because of the quality of what they produced. Blind people often had more acute abilities of hearing or other senses, so this was another reason to focus.

After a year at *Talking Books*, I found a different volunteer gig at *CRIS Radio for The Blind and Print Handicapped*. I recorded a weekly radio show of articles from the *Hartford Advocate*. I selected what I wanted to read from the paper and recorded it in a half-hour show. I loved it.

Occasionally, I'd get a voiceover gig from the advertising agency where I was employed. This helped me to build a portfolio and experience. Since then and over the years, I've been hired many times for many projects. I explored this skill for a while. I was afraid to try to have this be my sole occupation.

"You need something to fall back on," I heard echoes of my mother's childhood sentiment in my mind. There was too much uncertainty and competition.

I still enjoy voiceover work and get gigs from time to time. The last thing I recorded was a voiceover for the Hartford Public Library, for a fundraiser they were doing. I was happy to be hired and paid for the job.

I do have a responsibility with my skill. I have to ask myself on a regular basis: How can I be of further service to the world?

Every day, I have an opportunity to be of service: to be kind and loving and to choose peace. With my family, my community, my experiences. It doesn't always work. Many times, I fall short. I sometimes feel overwhelmed in my moment and I respond to life and others in a curt way. My work in this area is never done. Mindfulness and kindness are always needed.

Chapter Thirteen: Make it Better

♥

"And so, following these paths to truth,
we fit with the flow of the Kosmos,
we are delivered with currents that take us
outside of ourselves, beyond ourselves,
and force us to curb our self-serving ways,
as we fit into ever deeper and
wider circles of truth."

- Ken Wilber

Make it Better

When I was studying for my Master's, we talked about things like the cosmic energy of the universe, the creative intelligence, and being in the flow. Talking about this stuff and DOING them are different, aren't they? Just like the process of creating anything, we get to it by practicing it. We never arrive; we just keep going. My brain is constantly on me, talking about what I should write. I am not honoring it by letting it out. It is building up behind itself.

Progress and change require action. So much of my explorations in life happen in my mind, and the most important part of manifesting in the world is taking action. As they say in 12-step meetings, faith without works is dead.

I can believe all I want, but unless I do something about it, not much will happen. Life will still be happening and come at me, but I'm not providing any clearance to the universe and the divine to infuse my life. It requires action.

Serenity may seem like we should just sit there, but no. The peace comes after the work. It's like the feeling I get after a kick-ass boot camp class. There I am, immersed in group consciousness to help me push past my comfort zone, sweating and moving, past what I'd be capable of on my own. Then the class ends, and I am calmer, happier and more rested. After the workout, life feels better. To get to better, I have to accept the challenge. The only way out is through. Push, push, and push.

Someone once wrote that we experience life the way we experience our birth. If it is easy, there may be a sense of ease with your life. But I don't know that any life is comfortable. We all have to deal with loss and tragedy. None of us get out alive. It makes me wonder why my mind thinks there is something inherently wrong with a loss. Why do I avoid painful situations even though every time I face a challenge, I come out a stronger person with more insight, more wisdom and more compassion? That is the grace of the creative intelligence. It is the conscious evolution of my being. As I write, I stand on the shoulders of my artistic ancestors, and every author that started with pangs of doubt, inadequacy, and shame. Pushing past this obstacle is the great mystery of getting from stalling to doing, and getting in gear.

Towards the end of my drinking career, I thought I was in control and I could stop any time. I was just choosing not to. In reality, I couldn't and I wouldn't. It's funny how the mind plays tricks on the self that we think one thing but we're operating a different way. With the clarity of sobriety I can see with a different lens — the lens of the mind in full view with nowhere to hide.

I was what they call a high-bottom drinker and a high-functioning alcoholic. On the outside, you might see me have a too many glasses of wine at a party, but I was not sitting in the gutter in a trench coat clasping a paper bag with some drink in it. I ran businesses. I held high-powered advertising jobs, and I had some great relationships. It looked pretty good from a distance. But man was I in pain. Pain from unmanageability. Pain from a lack of life skills. I had no idea how to function when life happened. I just knew how to escape.

I'm starting to get comfortable with being uncomfortable. And that's a very uncomfortable place to be. So how do we resolve this? Healing work and sobriety looks at ways to ease the pain. Without drugs, without avoiding, just a little approaches to chip away at the monster that is our self-inflicted suffering.

Conclusion

The reflection artworks created during this time of healing were all self-portraits of some kind. I always see the artist in a work of art and in these I see myself.

Eliminating self-judgment and allowing the creative process to flow, I created a unique body of work that represents my personal experience of learning and transformation. It became a catalyst that informs future action. I can address any life issue by reflection, meditation and ultimately, creation. I can also heal life pain and other issues through art making.

When I show my artwork publicly, I share ideas for humanity and evolution. My artwork is a prayer and an outbound communication with the divine. My observers are witnesses and sometimes, active participants. This process is my conscious evolution in action.

My soul mission, as far as I am aware of it, is to inspire self-awareness for others and be of service in the world through conscious living. Before I can share what I need to teach, I must experience it within.

My exploration of art has brought me deeper into self. It allowed me to select ideas that resonate and require reflection and a way to access the divine.

If art can be a pathway to creative intelligence that exists in the universe, then we, as artists, can be channels. Perhaps that is why we are so captivated by the high-caliber work in museums and galleries. Artists are conduits for other dimension communications with our collective higher selves.

Change is a process, not an event. So is recovery. We don't arrive there. We do the best we can each day to become the best version of ourselves so we can help humanity. The whole point is to be of service to others and help them on their path. That is conscious evolution.

For my process to be potent, I had to get into 12-step work to clear away my self-delusions and deal with my alcoholism. The illness of alcoholism is permanent, so my recovery is a permanent process. So I have to keep going. Keep learning, keep growing, keep sharing and keep living. I want to relax into life and breathe through the hard parts. It's easier said than done. There will always be hard parts. If I am in the moment, all is well.

In caring for my 92-year old father in law, Paul, I've learned he is a miracle. His physical body is nearly a century old, and he has seen and experienced many things. He is wise and insecure at the same time. I see his vulnerabilities and wish he would let it all go and just live out loud. I want that for him because I want that for me. I see my reflection in him and realize that I have a whole lifetime ahead of me, perhaps. We never know when our last breath will come. We must see the miracles. We must live the wonders each and every day.

Our Still Waters neighbor Norm stopped by to visit. We were standing in front of our newly rebuilt main house. Tao had his shirt off, revealing his healed open-heart surgery scar from a scary and successful incident three years prior. Tao was looking lean from recent healthy weight loss. Norm exclaimed, "How many miracles are you going to have?"

We have had many. It's easier to see from the outside how many blessings are here. In a sense, life itself is a miracle. Waking up and breathing, heart beating, eyes open, senses functioning. It is so good to step outside of the drama of daily living and hover in a different dimension of existence. It is not always easy to stay in this place.

The other day, someone came up to me in a meeting and said, "Amy, you are always in beautiful places like Still Waters. How lucky!"

"Well, I responded, Still Waters is indeed beautiful, but there are a thousand tasks always waiting and beyond that a thousand more." She looked at me quizzically. I didn't explain it. I realized that it is Tao and my jobs as shepherds of that property to care for it. Others enjoy it. That is the deal.

Still Waters is a ton of work. We are always working the land, property and right now the business — to bring it back to life after the fire. On the outside, everyone sees beauty and calmness. For Tao and me, the property pushes us to prepare it for its work. We take every penny we earn in other businesses and put it into the revival of Still Waters. We are on a mission to re-open Still Waters, to facilitate its work for others.

Each year, we gather at Still Waters with family. Everyone comes out from California, some from Florida. We have been doing so for the past seven years when Tao and I began funding and owning the property.

At the moment of this writing, they are all here. Our crew includes my husband, father-in-law Paul, my mother-in-law Mavis from Florida and my husband's sister Zen from California and her family, including my brother-in-law Todd and three young nephews, Ben, Bodee and Bronson. The boys are chasing frogs as Zen cooks them quesadillas on the grill. Todd is working on his computer at the large outdoor dining table. After lunch, we are all going to paint Cottage Four Directions a contemporary grey. Zen has a conference call. Tao wants a nap. We are family here, doing happy family things. It moves me to think that this is my life now. It's very different from where I started.

Tao and his siblings are attached to Still Waters. They take the time and expense to bring their families here, to our Place of Peace Among the Pines to gather, laugh, work on the grounds and enjoy the sacred energy.

Even though the property was a construction site since the fire three and a half years ago, they still want to be here. It is far from perfect. Yet it is imperfectly perfect. We are experiencing the evolution of the property. The main house was partially rebuilt where the fire was. We have seven new bedrooms and four and a half new bathrooms. The house has all new plumbing and heating. The other day, we got running water once again. Yet no matter what we do to the main house or other buildings, the quiet sense of wonder and the energetic life of the grounds remains the same. I find that working on the grounds, shaping the landscape by mowing, weeding and planting, gives me a feeling of communing with nature.

We are co-creating. A core part of me wants to control everything and everyone. I want to tell everyone where to put their stuff and how to do things. The peace and serenity come in when I let go and release the need to control others. When I let them be how they want to be they show up even better than when I manage the situation.

Surrounded by family near the pond, I took a deep breath and walked to the porch of Cottage Duality so I could write. It takes just a minute to walk from the lake to Cottage Duality.

My creative outlet shifted from visual art making to writing. It has become a meditation and listening for clues. Writing gives me a feeling like nothing else does.

The sun was streaming through the trees, and a gentle yet firm, warm breeze billowed freely. As I walked, I felt an enormous sense of gratitude welling up in my soul. In this sacred moment, another profound sense of appreciation emerged. I am here in this beautiful, magnificent place. Tao and I have a lifetime of work ahead of us. In a direct experience of nature, a sense of God quietly whispers to me, it's okay. "I'm here. This is good. I'm with you, always."

I can think of no other place in the world that I would rather be.

❤

Acknowledgements

The first time I spoke with my husband, Tao LaBossiere, I called to talk to the director of Hartford ArtSpace Gallery. I wasn't sure how to pronounce Tao, as I had his name from an email. I learned it was pronounced "Dow" and that day I met the most generous, loving, creative and sincere man I have ever known. Tao is the love of my life and the one who supports and encourages my creativity every day. He lures me beyond my self-made limitations. Tao stretches me even when I don't want to be, as any good partner would do. He pushes my buttons and I grow softly (sometimes, not so softly!). We have been through so much already in our first decade together. My life would not be the same and this book would not be here without him.

Tao's family also had a profound influence on my development strides. Zen Honeycutt, my activist sister-in-law, is the most unstoppable woman I know. For seven years, Zen encouraged Tao and me to participate in the Landmark Forum. We finally did. Zen never gives up. Several years ago, Zen told Tao and me about how she wanted to get a bunch of moms together to march in 4th of July parades and raise GMO labeling awareness. Six months later, she had 177 groups marching across the nation united in a cause called Moms Across America. Zen taught me that anything is possible, we can be unstoppable and think big.

Paul LaBossiere is my third father in this lifetime, after my biological father Bill and my late stepfather Charlie. Paul is Tao's 92-year old dad, and has a remarkable life. He has wonderful stories, many achievements and raised a powerful family. With my mother-in-law Mavis, Paul created

Still Waters, his legacy and our retreat center. Paul built up the property when Tao, Zen, and Chi (Tao's other extraordinary sister) were kids. Together, they created an amazing life and business.

In the past several years, I've been helping Paul. Caring for him is what inspired me to start writing again. The writing voice became loud, and beckoned me until I began releasing it. I have had this creative pull before. At first, I was going to write a book about my experiences helping Paul. Perhaps I will do that next. But as I was starting to write more and more, this other creation of *Finding Still Waters* began to emerge. I was gently guided to realize that this would be my first book.

In his lifetime, Paul LaBossiere was a poet, fourth-grade teacher, seasoned actor, resort owner, Christian Science minister, salesman, navy seaman, inventor, stock boy, and father. I am grateful to know him and be part of his extended family.

My mother is a smart and tough New Yorker. She taught me the important life quality of never giving up. My father taught me to question everything and make sure it's credible. Charlie, my late stepfather, gave me my first glimpses at true love and creativity. Without all of them, I am certain this book would not exist.

Sometimes food changes everything — we change and then eat differently. Sometimes we eat differently and then we change. Either way, a profound shift happens. Corrina Richards, a yoga teacher in West Hartford, CT and holistic health coach, ran an online food detox program. I signed up while I was pursuing my Master's degree in Conscious Evolution. I made my first green smoothie during that program and it changed my life. A green drink intimidated me. It's like I could sense that change would come. From there, I developed my interest in health and nutrition, went on to study at the Institute for Integrative Nutrition (IIN) and became a certified holistic health coach. Years later, Corrina came to Still Waters and hosted two amazing yoga retreats with Kundalini yoga teacher Marcia Vallier. I don't know if Corrina knows the value she added to my life with her program. It changed me in unexpected ways.

Art, like love, will find us, even when we are not looking for it. Creativity, like love, longs to be expressed. My inner artist needed a way out. Over the years, several individuals and organizations were there for me when I found them. Jack Lardis, a former advertising executive, created Oil Drum Art (ODA), an organization that promotes oil drums as art canvases. I expressed my creativity with visual art, and a whole new world opened up to me. Jack gave me my first oil drum, the blank canvas for my first real work of art. It is also through ODA that I met Tao, the love of my life.

There are many evolutionaries on the path who brought me to next-level consciousness and soul-arising thinking. Some of these people I have met in person and others through their work, including Ken Wilber, through his books, articles, and videos. I continue to receive soul food from his teaching and influence. We have never met personally, but he is a philosopher that I deeply admire.

Bud Stone, founder of The Graduate Institute (TGI) also had a profound influence on this book. Bud created an educational institution that improves the world and helps people truly grow. Charles Silverstein was the coordinator for my graduate cohort, and overall Sherpa for the TGI program and Allan Combs was our academic director. All the presenters with the TGI program had a profound impact on my education and development. I have special gratitude for presenter Rose Sackey-Mulligan, who said, "We stand on the shoulders of our ancestors." That shook me to my core and my ancestors nod in agreement.

My gratitude and love occur more deeply in my soul because of Mata Amritanandamayi. Known around the world as Amma, she is a Hindu spiritual leader known as the "hugging saint." She is an amazing spiritual teacher and divine mother who blesses me with her hugs. Each time, she pulls my energy up another notch so that I can get closer to the presence of God. OM LOKAH SAMASTAH SUKHINO BHAVANTU — May all beings everywhere be happy.

Do people enter our lives for a reason? I'm not sure, but I know that they influence us. Evelyn Rysdyk, a shaman who lives in Maine, once gave me a part-time project that introduced me to Shamanism and launched me on a spiritual path. It might have been the most important moment of my life.

Chris Grosso, a modern-day philosopher, author, public speaker and kind-hearted soul helped me along the path as well. His work reminded me of my internal connection to the Conscious Evolution program. Chris and I had a pivotal phone conversation about writing and he pointed me to Jeff Brown (who I was already following on Facebook), a poignant writer and publisher. I jumped into Jeff's *Writing Your Way Home* course, which sparked the continuation of the journey — and ultimately the writing of this book.

I acknowledge my dear friend Christine Pallotti, who picked up the phone on a dark day and changed the course of my life at that moment. Special thanks to Emily L., who planted a seed with me about recovery at an art show many years ago.

My accountability partner, Brandi Blouch wrote her book at the same time. Brandi and I kept each other on track and had fun while doing it. Caresse Amenta, my amazing graphic designer, made this book beautiful.

My persistent editor Kim Julian pushed me beyond where I was comfortable. I am grateful to Nan Price, editor and queen of the red pen, along with Teresa Pelham and Valerie Popovich. And thanks to my beautiful mentor, Dr. Laura Shafer. This book would not exist in its current form without her guidance. Laura suggested that I write every day; she taught me much about being a grown up and embracing my true self.

Resources

Throughout my journey, I received great knowledge by participating in programs from a variety of organizations. Doing any kind of growth work is not always easy or fun, although sometimes it was. There were times of great laughter and moments of great peace. Even the hard work of the 12 steps in recovery has its shining moments. One of the most important things I learned through my participation is to have an open mind. Here are some questions that help me in this area.

• Am I willing to dig deep into the darkness of my soul to look at what is truly there?
• Can I listen to what others have to say about their path and what worked for them?
• Am I willing to do the hard work of healing?
• Can I be open to learning something new?
• Can I suspend my disbelief for a moment?
• Can I be okay with being wrong?
• Can I look at myself honestly?

The answers to these questions will change and shift over time. There are many more to ask. Here are some organizations to check out for more information:

The Graduate Institute. A state-accredited higher education institution focused on integrative and holistic studies Master's degree programs in Bethany, CT. My alma mater. *learn.edu*

Landmark Worldwide. A personal growth, training and development company for high-performing individuals who are ready to get out of their own way. I have taken many courses through Landmark and the most notable, The Landmark Forum. *Landmarkworldwide.com*

Institute for Integrative Nutrition. The world's largest nutrition school, headquartered in New York City, offers online learning. My alma mater. I am an Ambassador. *Integrativenutrition.com*

Alcoholics Anonymous. A 12-step focused, international & anonymous fellowship whose mission is "to stay sober and help other alcoholics achieve sobriety." *Aa.org*

Refuge Recovery. A mindfulness-based addiction recovery community that practices and utilizes Buddhist philosophy as the foundation of the healing process. *Refugerecovery.org*

Amma. Mata Amritanandamayi, known throughout the world as Amma, or Mother, offers selfless love and compassion toward all beings. She dedicates her entire life to alleviating the pain of the poor, and those suffering physically and emotionally. *Amma.org*

Additional Reading

These books were influential to my life. Many of them came to me through my work in the Conscious Evolution program. Check them out if you are inspired to.

Alcoholics Anonymous. New York, NY: Alcoholics Anonymous World Services, 1990.

Allen, Pat B. *Art Is a Way of Knowing.* Boston: Shambhala, 1995.

Allen, Pat B. *Art Is a Spiritual Path.* Boston: Shambhala, 2005.

Burroughs, Augusten. *Running with Scissors: A Memoir.* St. Martin's Press. 2002.

Cassou, Michele, and Stewart Cubley. *Life, Paint and Passion: Reclaiming the Magic of Spontaneous Expression.* New York: Jeremy P. Tarcher/Putnam, 1995.

Eisenstein, Charles. *The Yoga of Eating. Transcending Diets and Dogma to Nourish The Natural Self.* New Trends Publishing, Inc. 2003.

Elgin, Duane, and Deepak Chopra. *Living Universe.* Berrett-Koehler Publishers, 2009.

Csikszentmihalyi, Mihaly. *Flow: The Psychology of Optimal Experience.* New York: Harper Row, 2009.

Harner, Michael. *The Way of The Shaman.* Harper & Row. 1980.

Harvey, Andrew. *The Hope: A Guide to Sacred Activism.* Hay House, Inc. 2009

Grey, Alex, and Albert Hofmann. *Transfigurations: Alex Grey.* Rochester, Verm.: Inner Traditions International, 2001.

Laszlo, Ervin. *Science and the Akashic Field: An Integral Theory of Everything.* Rochester, VT: Inner Traditions, 2007.

Peat, F. David. *Gentle Action: Bringing Creative Change to a Turbulent World.* Pari: Pari Publishing, 2008.

Quinn, Daniel. *Ishmael.* New York: Bantam Books, 2017.

Rosado, Raul Quinones. *Consciousness-in-action: Toward an Integral Psychology of Liberation & Transformation.* Caguas, Puerto Rico: Publication, 2007.

Shlain, Leonard. *Art & Physics: Parallel Visions in Space, Time, and Light.* New York: William Morrow/HarperCollins, 2007.

Tarnas, Richard. *The Passion of the Western Mind: Understanding the Ideas That Have Shaped Our World View.* London: Pimlico, 2010.

Wilber, Ken. *A Brief History of Everything.* (2nd ed.). Shambhala. 2001.

About Still Waters

Nestled among 100 acres of conservation forest and a private, 12-acre pond, Still Waters is an artist-owned bed and breakfast retreat center in the Last Green Valley of Connecticut. Still Waters offers artfully appointed, clean, rustic and comfortable lodging. It has a newly built, year-round main house with five guest rooms, a master suite and an outdoor water-view dining deck. Two waterfront cottages and a five-bedroom guest house are open seasonally. A separate studio includes a massage room and is available for workshops. Close by the pond is a sunrise yoga deck and a natural spillway meditation swing. Guests can enjoy hiking the sculpture trail and viewing the colonial sawmill foundation and powerful waterfall dam originally built in the 1700s.

Since 1968, Still Waters hosted groups from all over the world, mostly the Tristate area but also as far as China. The LaBossiere family offered rustic, camp-style accommodations. In 2010, Tao and Amy LaBossiere re-launched Still Waters after 15-year hiatus. Tao and Amy were operating the business seasonally until a major house fire in the Spring of 2014 shut down the property. Part of the main house was deconstructed and rebuilt from 2016 to 2017.

Today, Still Waters provides accommodations for group leaders who want to organize their events at a beautiful healing location. Still Waters hosts our own monthly R&R retreats for individuals and couples providing them with a chance to unplug and relax in nature. As Still Waters continues its multi-year renovation and revitalization process, the accommodations will include overnight accommodations for up to 40 guests.

Still Waters is a woman-owned, husband-and-wife-run business, with Amy LaBossiere as managing partner and Tao LaBossiere as a partner. Tao is the visionary for the physical property and grounds, while Amy handles the business side. Their creative balance keeps the momentum going. Visit stillwaterspond.com for more information.

About the Author

Amy LaBossiere is an author, entrepreneur, and award-winning, intuitive conceptual artist. A driven small business owner and creative thinker, Amy has a long-lived hobby of acting and voiceover work. She is managing partner of Still Waters Bed and Breakfast Retreat Center and Administrative Director of Art of Tao LaBossiere LLC. She is also a marketing consultant and health coach. Amy volunteers as co-director of Hartford ArtSpace Gallery.

Amy holds a Bachelor's of Fine Arts in Communication Arts with a specialization in public relations from Long Island University/CW Post; a Master of Arts in Conscious Evolution from The Graduate Institute; and a certificate in Holistic Health Coaching from The Institute for Integrative Nutrition. She coaches clients individually and helps group leaders plan their holistic retreats and retreat menus. Amy also designs and manages the monthly R&R retreats at Still Waters.

As a visual artist, Amy began her art career in 2003 when inspired by an oil drum as a canvas. Since then, she created numerous works of outsider art per year — some award-winning pieces and purchased for private collections. Amy exhibited her artwork in more than 50 group art exhibitions over the past 14 years throughout Connecticut and New York. She had a solo art show, Conscious Evolution: Reflections on a Master's Program in 2011.

As a writer, Amy burned all her journals in 1996 during her first marriage. She put them all in a fish tank and lit them up on a back porch of a condo where she was living. Over the years, Amy wrote for newspapers, magazines and was a copywriter for businesses. She began writing for her own creativity in 2016.

Amy is a dual resident of Hartford and Voluntown, CT with her husband and business partner, award-winning artist Tao LaBossiere. They have two rescue dogs, a miniature poodle named BeeBe and a black lab named Maggie.

This is Amy's first book.

CPSIA information can be obtained
at www.ICGtesting.com
Printed in the USA
LVOW13s1359230318
570964LV00013B/181/P